SPLENDOUR AT COURT

Dressing for Royal Occasions since 1700

SPLENDOUR AT COURT

Dressing for Royal Occasions since 1700

NIGEL ARCH
AND
JOANNA MARSCHNER

UNWIN HYMAN

London   Sydney

First published in Great Britain by Unwin Hyman,
an imprint of Unwin Hyman Limited, 1987.

Unwin Hyman Limited, Denmark House,
37–39 Queen Elizabeth Street, London SE1 2QB
and
40 Museum Street, London WC1A 1LU

Allen & Unwin Australia Pty Ltd
8 Napier Street, North Sydney, NSW 2060, Australia

Allen & Unwin
with the Port Nicholson Press,
PO Box 11-838 Wellington, New Zealand.

ISBN 0 7135 26610

British Library Cataloguing in Publication Data

Arch, Nigel
  Splendour at court.
  1. Great Britain—Court and courtiers
  2. Great Britain—History—18th century
  3. Great Britain—History—19th century
  4. Great Britain—History—20th century
  I. Title II. Marschner, Joanna
  942.07   DA28.1
  ISBN 0–7137–2661–0

Designed by Malcolm Harvey Young
Printed in Great Britain
by Scotprint Ltd, Musselburgh

NOTE Any views expressed in this book are those of the
authors and not those of the Department of the
Environment.

CONTENTS

A *Punch* cartoon 22 May 1929, illustrating the perils of waiting in one's car in the queue along the Mall before an Evening Court.

Enterprising Hawker. "BUY A NICE BLOOD ORANGE, LADY; ALL SWEET AND JUICY."

CHAPTER ONE

'Passport into Good Society'

The Nature and Function of the Court

This is a book about a lost world, one that vanished nearly fifty years ago. The last time debutantes, girls who had attended the round of parties and receptions that made up the Season, were presented to a British sovereign at an Evening Court, was just before the Second World War. The last Levee, the reception for gentlemen, held by the King at St James's Palace was also in 1939.

Presentations, at Afternoon Parties at Buckingham Palace, continued for some years after the war but these were occasions of a different character and the dresses worn to them of a different style, to the glittering Evening Courts and resplendent Court Dresses of the earlier era. Dresses, worn with feather and veil headdresses and embroidered and sequinned trains suspended from the shoulders, now survive as museum pieces, or perhaps still lie neglected in family attics. One may catch a glimpse of the magnificence of court uniforms which were worn at Levees and Evening Courts at some of the great state occasions, such as the State Opening of Parliament. Here the Queen is preceded in her procession by the Lord Great Chamberlain wearing his uniform coat of scarlet wool, richly embroidered with gold lace, and followed by Royal Pages of Honour whose costume owes more to the eighteenth than the twentieth century.

The pomp and circumstances of Royal ceremonial is a rare sight today but the world that this book will examine is a far stranger one. In an increasingly informal society, in which many social barriers have been broken down it is arresting to read of the rigid code of manners which once determined who was and who was not eligible to be received at Court, and who was or was not therefore part of 'Good Society'.

Percy Armytage, who served as a courtier under both Edward VII and George V recalled that he had always understood the word Society – the capital S is important — to mean only those people who were eligible for presentation at Court and that, for example, barristers of good family were received but not solicitors.

Correct dress was as important as the right background. George V is said to have been such a zealous guardian of correct form that even members of his Household took great care to check their attire before entering the Royal presence.

The clothes that this book will describe and illustrate and the etiquette which will emerge from memoirs and books of instruction will undoubtedly strike the modern reader from time to time as extraordinary. It is important therefore to remember that within those clothes there lived and breathed people whose virtues and faults were in many ways our own. For example it was quite possibly simple envy that led Mrs Delany to describe Lady Carteret's dress in 1741 as 'an ugly flowered silk on a dirty yellow ground'.

We shall meet Mrs Delany again, usually in more generous mood. She is an invaluable source for the student of eighteenth-century dress. A comfortably off, twice married lady whose own skills as an embroiderer gave her the sharp eye for detail and style that enables us, over two hundred years later, to picture the magnificent court gowns she saw, and on occasion wore.

It is important at the outset to make clear that we are concerned with a particular type of clothing—that worn to the Royal Court in Britain. An understanding of the nature of the Court is consequently crucial. The Court was

THE LAST EVENING COURT OF 1939
An anonymous photograph of this historic event showing, on the right, debutantes, in the centre the King and Queen (seated) and, amongst the crowd, the distinctive plumes of the Gentlemen at Arms.

and is identified with the Royal Family, but we are not interested here in royal clothing as such, only in as much as it was worn to Court. What King George III wore to the Court held on his birthday is therefore to be found in these pages (his outfit included a coat with diamond buttons), but not the cloth and cut of his nightshirt.

What was the Court? In one sense the answer to this question is simply the king or queen's residence, but for us bricks and mortar are less important than people and occasion. Court dress and etiquette were a part of the life of the people who surrounded the monarch, the Royal Household and the various assemblies held by the Royal Family.

The Royal Household consists of officers responsible for aspects of Royal life, for example the public or ceremonial and the domestic. The

great officers of state ultimately responsible for these functions are the Lord Chamberlain and the Lord Steward. Since this book is concerned with the public life of the Court, it is with the ramifications of the Lord Chamberlain's Office that it will from time to time be concerned.

A description of the office is included in a book published in 1838 written by William Thoms, a Fellow of the Society of Antiquaries of London, entitled *The Book of the Court*.

Thoms found a reference to the office of Lord Chamberlain as far back as 1208, although there is little doubt that an officer with the Lord Chamberlain's responsibilities was a part of the king's entourage from a much earlier date. During the Middle Ages this officer wielded real political power, endorsing bills and petitions to the king and controlling access to the monarch.

8

Even after the changes in the organization of government that took place under the Tudor dynasty, the Lord Chamberlain was not a figure to be overlooked in political or social matters. His powers of patronage did not slip away until the eighteenth century. These powers depended in part on the great number of positions at Court which he controlled, ranging from grooms and ushers upwards to his deputy, the Vice Chamberlain. Lord Hervey, who occupied this post during the reign of George II, claimed that he had brought about the promotion of his father's chaplain to Dean and then Bishop of Norwich. A bill introduced by Burke, when it became law in 1782, cut down the number of offices, and consequently the patronage that could be dispensed but even when Thoms was writing the Lord Chamberlain controlled a considerable number of officers and servants 'above

stairs'. His appointment only ceased to be political, changing with each government, during the present century.

Some of the Lord Chamberlain's advisers were concerned with the regulation of clothing to be worn at Court. From the nineteenth century onwards greater restrictions than had been in force before were applied to the type of person who could be received and what should be worn. In 1882 a book entitled *Dress Worn at Court*, drew together the pronouncements that had been made in previous years and later editions included specifications for ladies dress, even concerning the colour of gloves to be worn.

The Courts at which our predecessors had to be careful about the colour of their gloves (and as we shall see the degree of *décolletage* on the dress) were the assemblies that had been held by

A queue of debutantes with other guests outside Buckingham Palace, 21 March 1956. The feathers and trains of the pre-War Courts have disappeared to be replaced by afternoon dress.

the sovereign or members of his family for hundreds of years. They were a very important part of the social calendar, and for many years attendance at them was vital to politicians as well as socialites. Robert Walpole the first head of a British government to bear the title Prime Minister, was of the opinion that it was not possible to carry on 'the King's business', by which he meant the government of the country, unless you could demonstrate to potential supporters and allies that you enjoyed the favour of the Court.

Although as we have suggested this political aspect of the Court was to wane, social advantage was always to be gained. Swift remarked that 'The Court serves me for a coffee-house once a week', while Lady Violet Greville writing in 1892 in *The Gentlewoman in Society*,

recorded that 'Very very few indeed there are who have not wished the Queen to confer the final touch upon entrance into the great world'. She meant presentation, at a levee if you were a gentleman, or a Drawing Room, if you were a lady.

However Lady Violet bemoaned the incursion into Court of 'people of no estimation except in their own', and contrasted this contemporary decadence of manners with the practice and aspiration of a generation earlier, when nobody thought of attending Court unless their position demanded it or they required 'that passport of admittance into Good Society' which presentation supplied, for example if travelling abroad and therefore needing to impress foreigners that one was indeed a gentleman or lady. Whether Lady Greville was correct

THE STATE OPENING OF PARLIAMENT 1970
Court uniforms on parade include those of the Yeomen of the Guard who
line the route, the Royal Pages of Honour holding the Queen's train and the
Lord Great Chamberlain (with his back to the camera), in a scarlet coat with
gold embroidery.

in her estimation of her contemporaries is argu-
able but she certainly summed up what going to
Court in the nineteenth century was all about—
social prestige.

The Drawing Room was held in the afternoon during Queen Victoria's reign and
although its timing was altered by her son,
Edward VII, to the evening, the Evening Courts
of his reign and afterwards performed basically
the same function.

If at all familiar with the term, most people
will think of a drawing room as a chamber in a
house, perhaps a slightly grand one. This meta-
morphosis from architectural concept to social
event occurred during the eighteenth century.
The drawing room, (originally known as the
withdrawing room) was a chamber in which the
king could receive people, who were therefore
distinguished from those who were restricted to

the more public rooms. Being in the drawing
room meant that you were 'in' socially. It is said
that Queen Charlotte, King George III's consort, was the first Queen to place on a regular
basis the practice of having girls presented to
her at the Drawing Room, a sign that they had
entered Society. From 1837 these girls, or
young ladies as they were more properly
known, were often called debutantes, later
shortened to debs.

The Levee, at one time a term for a morning
assembly held by an important person, be it
landowner, politician or prince, in the course of
the eighteenth century came to mean the occasion for gentlemen to be presented to the king.
The Court and Country Companion, published
shortly before Queen Victoria's accession to the
throne says that 'noblemen, gentlemen and
clergy, receiving state, naval, military, legal,

civil or ecclesiastical appointments from the crown are usually presented at His Majesty's Levee'.

The *Companion*, a very useful guide to the fledgeling courtier, gave elaborate instructions as to the procedure to be adopted to secure a principal role in this rite. This involved, above all, knowing someone who had already been presented, since only they could act as sponsor to one's own application. The same applied to the Drawing Room. If not already acquainted with a suitable person all was not necessarily lost. It is reported that some members of the aristocracy who had been presented would act as sponsors in return for financial remuneration.

The rigid regulation of attendance at Court was not always a feature of the social scene. Dudley Ryder, a young lawyer in London, in 1715 recorded that on one occasion having decided to go to a ball held at St James's Palace and being without a ticket he gained admittance by the simple expedient of pressing a shilling into the doorman's hand.

It is important to recall that Ryder put on his best clothes as he had at least to look like someone who should be admitted, even if in the event a shilling had to be employed to assist entry. This appreciation that court dress had to be special, and costly, runs through the whole history of the subject, impervious to changing manners.

Spencer Cowper told Lady Cowper in 1722 that his daughter could not go to the Prince of Wales's Birthday Court 'for I think it better not

THE MARRIAGE PROCESSION AND CEREMONY
One of a set of three engravings of the marriage procession of Queen Victoria in 1840, depicting various members of the Royal Household.

Gent. Usher of the Black Rod. *Sir A. Clifford.* — Garter K. at Arms. *Sir W. Woods.* — Earl Marshal. *Duke of Norfolk.* — H.R.H. Princess Sopha. Matila. of Gloster. — Princess Auga. of Cambridge. — Hon. Miss

Lady Augusta Somerset. — H.R.H. The Duchess of Kent. — Lady F. Howard. — H.R.H. The Princess Augusta.

Knesebeck. — Duke of Sussex. — Col. Wildman. — Vice Chamberlain. — Lord Melbourne. — Lord Chamberlain. — THE QUEEN. — Lady A. Paget. — Lady C. Lennox. — Lady

Groom of the Robes. *Capt. Seymour.* — Master of the Horse. *Lord Albermarle.* — Mistress of the Robes. *Duchess of Sutherland.* — Marchs. of Normanby. — Duchess of Bedford. — Countss. of Charlemont. — Countss. of

to attempt it without doing it as it ought to be'. Mrs Spencer whom Mrs Delany spotted at Court in 1756 clearly followed this principle for 'she went to Court in white and silver, as fine as brocade and trimming could make it ... the diamonds worth twelve thousand pounds, her earrings three drops, all diamonds, no paltry scrolls of silver'. Descendants of these fine ladies at Queen Victoria's Drawing Rooms were no different in their desire to display their wealth, since the dress that the Baroness de Goltstein wore in May 1894, was obviously costly: 'Corsage and petticoat of cream satin with Brussels lace fastened with bunches of daffodils; train of brocade with a design of daffodils on green satin ground and lined with yellow duchesse, coming from both shoulders'.

By this time gentlemen accompanying their ladies to the Drawing Room, or attending a Levee, would have had no reason to be ignorant of what was appropriate clothing. The nineteenth-century Court, insofar as male dress is

QUEEN VICTORIA'S JUBILEE DRAWING ROOM May 1887
The Lord Chamberlain is shown reading out the name of the debutante who is kissing the hand of the Princess of Wales.

LORD MIDDLETON
Painted by Sir Joshua Reynolds in 1762, Lord Middleton is shown wearing the Coronation robes of a Baron. The suit includes a coat of silk brocade and breeches of red velvet.

14

Miss Ruby Ray photographed in court dress with the obligatory feather and
veil head-dress, court train and white kid gloves in 1906.

JOHN LORD HERVEY C 1730
Attributed to Fayram. Regarded by some of his contemporaries as an
effeminate poseur, Hervey's memoirs are a rich source for the historian.

concerned, witnessed the triumph of uniform over individual magnificence. The peacock male of the Hanoverian Court, whose finery demonstrated to the world his leisured existence, far removed from any suggestion of manual labour, was transmuted into the official whose job required him to wear a predetermined form of dress to Court. There had been uniforms or liveries at Court for hundreds of years—the accounts of the Wardrobe Department refer to liveries for the Yeomen of the Guard and the Children of the Chapel Royal at St James's. But it was not until about 1820 that civil servants and members of the Household were to find themselves encased in uniforms richly ornamented with gold lace, the width of decoration indicating the rank of the man within it. His personality to that extent was enveloped in his uniform.

Going to court, in uniform or the embroidered silk coats of the earlier period, was clearly an experience to be savoured. It was not always the glittering affair that the breathless descriptions of the clothing might lead one to imagine. Fanny Burney, who served at the Court of George III, complained of the long hours one was expected to stand still in the King's presence. She was not even allowed to sneeze, while poor Mrs Spencer hurt her foot from too much standing about at Court, her shoe buckle being too tight.

Standing in what must have at times been a very embarrassed silence was not at all unusual. The Courts of Queen Anne seem to have been particularly prone to this form of social paralysis. Swift recorded that on one occasion there were so few present at the Drawing Room that the Queen sent for the company to come to her

TRAINING SCHOOL FOR LADIES ABOUT TO APPEAR AT COURT
A *Punch* cartoon June 1875, showing aspiring debutantes being put through their paces so they may cope with the ordeal of presentation.

bedchamber. Twenty courtiers stood around the Queen while she looked at them and they bowed to her. A few, a very few words were spoken, the Queen holding her fan to her face. At last, after what must have seemed to those present to be an eternity, the Queen announced it was time for dinner and left.

Perhaps the Queen failed to inject the requisite amount of life into her Courts because she was too concerned with checking that the correct rules and precedence were followed. The Duchess of Marlborough was of this opinion, although after their famous quarrel the Duchess cannot be thought of as an impartial judge of her one time friend. The Queen certainly knew when the wrong wig was being worn to Court. She observed Lord Bolingbroke incorrectly dressed and snapped that she supposed the next time his lordship appeared at Court it would be in his nightcap.

Court ceremony extended even to Royal attendance at church. Cesar de Saussure writing in *A Foreign View of England in the Reigns of George* I *and George* II describes going to the Chapel Royal at St James's. Six Yeomen of the Guard were on duty and they processed to the Chapel followed by a number of Gentlemen of the Household, including the Lord Chamberlain and the Master of the Household (who worked under the Lord Steward). Both of these officers carried white wands as emblems of their position. Behind them came two sergeants at arms carrying maces, then the sword of state born by a nobleman, followed by the King accompanied by the three eldest daughters of the Prince of Wales. Each of these girls had a squire in

attendance and the trains of their dresses were
carried by pages of honour. Concluding the
procession were ten Gentlemen Pensioners, a
Royal Bodyguard formed in the sixteenth century now known as the Gentlemen at Arms.

At two o'clock that afternoon there was a
Drawing Room. De Saussure observed the circle of people surrounding the King. The King
spoke with a few of the representatives of
foreign governments who were present, and
nodded to the young ladies. Apparently there
were more of these 'ornaments to society', as de
Saussure describes the ladies, present at the

week day Drawing Rooms, which were more
enjoyable as a result.

Reading accounts of receptions at Court during the nineteenth century and bearing in mind
the increasing care with which applications to
attend were scrutinized, it is the numbers which
impress. Perhaps this was the result of greater
wealth, giving more people the opportunity to
aspire to the social distinction offered by the
Court.

Richard Rush, American Minister to the
Court of St James has left a fascinating account
of his reception at a Levee held by the Prince

Regent at Carlton House in February 1818. Rush computed that a thousand people must have passed by the Prince, and he later compared the lines of gentlemen to a current flowing through the rooms.

A few weeks later Rush attended the first Drawing Room held by the Queen after the untimely death in childbirth of the Princess Charlotte, only offspring of the ill-fated union between the Prince Regent and Caroline of Brunswick. Passing through a gate on Constitution Hill and on to Hyde Park, Rush found the way lined with carriages at the side of the road, filled with people whose express purpose was to look at those bound for Court. Such scenes became commonplace during the Season, as carriages queued for the entrance to Buckingham Palace where the Drawing Rooms and the later Evening Courts were held. *Punch*, the humorous magazine which often found inspiration in the etiquette and clothing associated with the Court, painted a picture of Piccadilly

during the Season on 1863, where several miles of carriages are at a 'dead stop . . . each full of people eager to get to the Palace', while the public walks up and down on each side, freely criticizing the appearance of the ladies. These queues continued into the age of the motor car. One deb recalled sitting in her grandmother's car in the Mall, with the crowds watching.

Once inside the Palace the British skill in organizing and running ceremonial asserted itself. Each lady had a presentation card, on which was written her name. Leaving the line of other debutantes who were waiting to curtsey before the King and Queen she entered the Throne Room. Almost always all went well but on one occasion at least, between the wars, chaos threatened to break into the carefully orchestrated proceedings. It was clearly essential that the names as they were called out should match the debs as they walked forward to curtsey. Alas, one deb accidentally put her foot through the train of the girl in front of her.

22

A CORRECT REPRESENTATION OF THE
COMPANY GOING TO AND RETURNING
FROM HIS MAJESTY'S DRAWING·ROOM AT
BUCKINGHAM PALACE. An engraving
published by G Humphrey 25 May
1822.

Court dress c 1860. Made of cream silk
embroidered with a design of roses,
the dress has a train measuring eleven
feet which fastens at the waist.

The young lady could not face appearing before her sovereign with a damaged train and left hurriedly, so causing the order of names to be disrupted. The implications were ghastly—debs being presented under the incorrect name. Fortunately the Lord Chamberlain swiftly realized the mistake and the elegant, balletic ceremony continued, only slightly ruffled.

Although much was radically changed by the First World War, the Season of parties and presentations was soon re-established. It was to be the Second World War that curtailed forever the Evening Court and Levee. Afternoon-Presentation Parties began in 1947, but in November 1957 the Lord Chamberlain's Office announced that there would be no more of these after the following year and that additional Garden Parties would be held, so that larger numbers of the Queen's subjects could be invited to Buckingham Palace. At the last Pres-

Sir Robert Whigham and family 1933
The photograph shows Sir Robert in full dress military uniform and the ladies in court dress which includes the regulation feather and veil head-dresses, gloves and trains.

COUNTESS OF CALEDON. LADY FRANCES BALFOUR. DUCHESS OF BEDFORD. GEORGINA COUNTESS OF DUDLEY.

The Queen Magazine 1902
Illustration showing the court dresses worn by the Countess Caledon, Lady
Frances Balfour, the Duchess of Bedford and Georgina Countess of Dudley.

entation of all a young man is said to have
driven past the line of girls outside the Palace
displaying a placard upon which was written
'Farewell dear debs'.

The debs have not in fact disappeared from
the social landscape. There is still a Season
which is now divorced from the Court. Yet the

memories of an earlier age linger on, triggered
by the sight of court uniforms seen on State
occasions. Some dresses survive and the
thoughts of people who attended Court decades
ago are preserved. This book gives life to that
past. The story begins at the Court of Queen
Anne.

CHAPTER TWO

'A Great Deal of Finery'

The Eighteenth Century

On the fifth of August 1711 Jonathan Swift, later famous as the author of *Gulliver's Travels*, but at the time an Irish cleric with considerable social ambition prepared for Court. He shaved, dressed and set out for the Court which he equated with a coffee house. His record of three years attendance at the Royal Court, contained in a series of letters to two Irish ladies in Dublin, provides us with a lively insight into the manners and functions of the Court of Queen Anne.

Swift had been commissioned to plead the cause of the distressed Irish clergy to influential persons in England. The one place he could be sure of making the necessary contacts was at Court. Although never presented to the Queen, Swift was a frequent and sharp, observer and critic of the many dramas and comedies played out at the Drawing Rooms and Birthday Courts.

At Court political and social gossip was exchanged, favours sought, flattery dispensed on a prodigal scale and patronage given in exchange. Swift after an early enthusiasm for the business eventually became tired of the proceedings and intrigues. This is an indication of his misanthropy which coloured later comments in his correspondence, so that by December of 1712 he confesses that he was beginning to harbour a dislike of 'the course of public Affairs'.

Without appreciating the political, financial and social importance of the Court it is difficult to understand why men and women dressed in the fantastic costumes and performed the extraordinary rituals and evolutions that comprised Court life. The witnesses we shall call upon to help paint a picture of the Court between roughly 1700 and 1820 fall into two broad categories. First there are those men of affairs who were so preoccupied with the workings of the Court that they seem to have had little time to notice what was being worn. Second there are those whose memories of the Drawing Room and the Birthday Courts while providing us with a series of the most colourful and splendid images, do not permit analysis of the political science of the Georgian Court. Putting the two together provides a context in which to place the extraordinary confections of silk, lace and embroidery that yet survive.

Swift for example is always quick off the mark to alert his friends in Dublin to the news of who is in favour and who is not at Court. On 13 May 1711 he says that the Court was very full, as people expected to learn that Mr Harley would be made Earl of Oxford on being given the position of Lord Treasurer. Ten days later he was indeed created a peer and the Queen had 'a rod for him in her closet this week', a reference the ladies to whom he wrote would have understood to refer not to some chastisement the good earl was to suffer but rather the rod of office of Lord Treasurer which the Queen was to pass to him.

Swift was however not as close to the centre of events as others. John Lord Hervey, Vice Chamberlain in the Royal Household of George II and Queen Caroline, had ample opportunity of seeing the intricate machinery of Court intrigue at work, and on occasion to tinker with it himself. His memoirs, entitled *Some material towards Memoirs of the Reign of King George II* covers the 1730's very well. As Vice Chamberlain one of his duties was to keep the King and Queen fully informed about the proceedings of the Houses of Parliament. The King soaked up this information. On one occasion his appetite for Hervey's reports prevented the courtier from satisfying his own, as he kept Hervey

QUEEN ANNE AND THE KNIGHTS OF THE GARTER
In this painting by Peter Angelis (1713) Queen Anne is depicted receiving a
new knight at this elaborate court ceremony.

without dinner until three in the morning giving accounts of the day at Westminster. He was also literally privy to backstairs gossip since his lodgings at St James's Palace were at the foot of the Queen's Apartments. He was much more than a gossip columnist. Gossip at Court could equate with political power.

At Court Hervey would often discuss with Walpole, the King's first minister, matters of state and the way shifting allegiances in Parliament might work for or against a piece of government legislation. He appreciated fully the intricate negotiations that went on in 1733/4 over the succession to the post of Master of the Horse. Even today this official plays a vital part in the practical arrangements of the monarch's life. In the eighteenth century he could also expect to reap considerable financial reward. In

A VIEW OF THE BALL AT ST JAMES'S ON THE KING'S BIRTHDAY JUNE 4 1782
An engraving published in *The Lady's Magazine*.

1716 James Cathcart called it 'the handsomest employment in Britain'. In late 1733 two men were after the job and its perks—the Duke of Richmond and Lord Pembroke. Clearly both could not be successful, but Walpole was concerned to put both men in his debt by satisfying them. His elegant solution was to arrange for Lord Godolphin to relinquish the position of Groom of the Stole, on condition certain arrangements were made about the inheritance of his title, and to place the unsuccessful candidate for the Mastership in that post. The problem was that the King, who had to give his blessing to the arrangements, harboured an intense dislike of Godolphin's wife, and was reluctant to help the family in any way. Walpole was a man of great persuasive powers however and all was managed to his design, although the King complained 'You are always teasing me to do things that are disagreeable to me and for people I dislike'.

This neatly demonstrates the political necessity of what Hervey calls 'dangling after a court'. For those who knew their way around the metaphorical and literal corridors of powers in Royal palaces there was, power, influence and money to be found. It was a complex business, as Lord Chesterfield advised his son in 1753 'the links that form the court chain are innumerable and inconceivable'.

Politics was one magnet that attracted people to Court; social ambition was another. Lady Sarah Lennox writing in 1818 and commenting upon the Drawing Rooms that were by then held four times a year says that 'everyone man or woman that assumes the names of gentlemen

or lady go'. Presentation to the King or Queen conferred that special Royal seal of approval not to be found elsewhere and moreover, important in the era of the Grand Tour, was the sole passport to attendance at foreign courts.

The company which attended Court was both select and numerous, if we are to believe contemporary descriptions. The select quality derived from the wealth and connection perceived as necessary by those who attended, and the company was numerous because the Court was felt to be important. One of those who developed a taste for the contents of this honey pot was Lady Mary Coke, who was presented in 1766, at St James's Palace. After the Drawing Room she was sent for and both the King and the Queen were very gracious. She continued in this favoured state the following year when the king 'was particularly gracious and civil' to her in January at Court. It was an uncertain world however, as easy to fall from grace as to attain it, for in February poor Lady Coke confides 'I did not think the king so gracious to me as he sometimes is'. An adjective which recurs time and again in descriptions of the Court is fine. Mrs Delany says that there was 'a great deal of finery', the company was fine, the clothes fine. In one letter she remarks that she grows weary of employing the adjective, but apparently runs out of any others as she closes her letter soon after. Even when not fine there was usually something to note. For example on Monday 5 June 1769 there was 'not much finery' at the Birthday Court, but you could still look at the Queen's diamonds, the numbers and size of which surprised everyone.

Mantua and petticoat c 1745 of scarlet
ribbed silk embroidered with silver
threads. The hoop supporting the
petticoat would have measured six feet
across at its widest point.

Mantua and petticoat c 1750. Cream
silk brocaded with coloured silks and
silver thread. The lappets are of
Valenciennes lace.

A LADY IN THE COURT DRESS OF THE
YEAR 1770.
A contemporary engraving.

The Royal Family was at the centre of the Court. The character of the Court was therefore partly determined by the monarch and his or her family. Queen Anne was noted for the extreme dullness of her Court, and the rigidity with which she conducted it. This must have been partly a reflection of her almost constant illnesses, her life being plagued with miscarriages and gout. But she was at the same time a prisoner of the baroque tradition of court life, which emphasized the ritual and ceremony in the monarch's life.

For example when dressing the Queen, a lady of the bedchamber and a woman of the bedchamber had to be present. The woman would hand to the lady the Queen's shift and the lady would assist the Queen in putting it on. Similarly the Royal fan would be passed from the woman to a lady and then to the Queen, and another lady of the bedchamber would assist the Queen in putting her gloves on. Washing was even more complicated. The basin and ewer had to be brought into the Queen's bedchamber by a Page of the Backstairs, but he could not pour

the water over the Royal hands, an operation reserved for a woman of the bedchamber. He, and only he, was allowed to help the Queen put her shoes on.

George I brought a relaxation of such formality and gave to the eighteenth century a tradition of a more informal Court. This was of course comparative and must be set against the French Court in which the conduct of virtually every moment of the king's waking life was determined by one ritual or another from the *petit lever* when certain courtiers assisted with his ablutions, through the day including the *debotter*, the removing of the Royal boots, to the *coucher* and *petit coucher* when the monarch was put to bed.

Although more informal than courts of a similar size and importance abroad, the Hanoverian Court was impressive. Usually when Royalty was present there would be no chairs provided so that no one committed the solecism of sitting in the King's presence. At a Drawing Room a circle of persons usually formed and the King or Queen would move around the inside

A GENTLEMAN AND LADY IN THE COURT
DRESS OF THE YEAR 1771
A contemporary engraving.

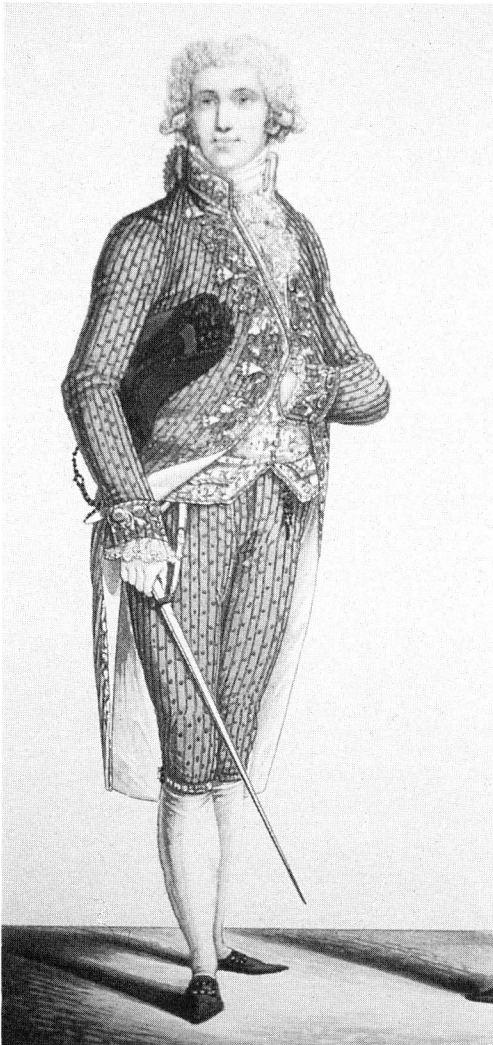

Heideloff's Gallery of Fashion Fashion
plate April 1796. The coat and
breeches are striped pink and black
and embroidered with gold, and the
white waistcoat has corresponding
gold embroidery.

Court dress c 1775. Pale green silk brocaded with coloured silks and metal threads. The dress is cut with a sack back and to accommodate wide hoops.

circumference exchanging a few words here and there. It was important to remember that one could not change the subject of conversation, but always let the Royal lead it. When talking to others, a mastery of the art of forms of conversation was essential. Lord Chesterfield advised his son 'there is a court jargon, a chit chat, a small talk, which turns upon trifles . . . it is the proper language of levees, drawing rooms and ante-chambers, it is necessary to know it'. Into this conversation, were one talking to 'useful persons' one would introduce that most useful weapon in the armoury of the courtier—flattery. Chesterfield tells his son 'Flattery, though a base coin, is the necessary pocket money at court; where by custom and consent it has obtained such currency that it is no longer a fraudulent but legal payment'.

A great deal of time was spent simply standing around. This was particularly the case with members of the Royal Household, whose duties required them to attend upon the King or Queen at the Drawing Room. On such occasions it was important not to be conspicuous in any way, and to prevent oneself from sneezing or coughing. Fanny Burney set down in December 1785 the way to behave. It was, she says, better to choke rather than cough, hold one's breath or break a blood vessel rather than sneeze. If a hairpin should prove painful it was not to be removed and if the agony became unbearable it was permitted to bite the inside of the cheek, providing that should a piece of flesh detach itself in the process it was shallowed, as spitting was certainly not allowed at court.

If you were not flattering, being flattered, talking to the King or Queen or biting the inside of your cheek, you might be dancing, as at the King's Birthday Ball. Here too there were strict rules of precedence to be observed— partners taking to the floor in order of rank and gentlemen being sure to hand their swords to the Lord Chamberlain before dancing.

Whether performing a minuet at a Birthday Ball or circulating amongst important contacts at a Drawing Room, the ladies and gentlemen were performing the roles for which their station in life had prepared them. They wore such costumes as would be appropriate to a world of ceremony, formal expensive clothes that were distinguished in a variety of ways from the fashionable dresses and suits worn

elsewhere. Even to observers at the time, some ladies went a little too far in the splendour of their dresses. Mrs Delany's sharp eye spied out Lady Huntingdom at the Birthday Court for the Prince of Wales in 1738. 'Most extraordinary' is her considered opinion, (a view with which one is inclined to concur) as the pattern on the dress was so elaborate that it would have been more appropriate for a 'stucco staircase than the apparel of a lady', who was 'a mere shadow that tottered under every step she took under the load'.

During the greater part of the eighteenth century the court dress style for ladies was the mantua and petticoat. The mantua entered the vocabulary of dress history in the mid-seventeenth century. From the early eighteenth century it was accepted as suitable dress for wear at Court. It was worn with a stomacher in front, and draped open to reveal a decorative petticoat beneath. Although always trained it was usual, at certain periods at least, for ladies to wear the train looped up. This was certainly true in the 1780's, when Sophie von La Roche was helping her friend Countess Reventlow, wife of the Danish Ambassador to the Court of St James's, dress for court. Her knowledge of the French Court enabled her to pinpoint a crucial difference in the regulations applied to ladies dress in the two countries. 'The train which at Versailles trails as a mark of respect is here held up for the same reason.'

It would be incorrect however to say that the style was consistent throughout the period. Mrs Delany writing of a Birthday Court of 1754 says that before it she visited some friends and one of the ladies was trying on her dress and jewels and 'practised dancing with her train'. In 1777 the *Magazine à la Mode* reports that when the ladies danced minuets they let their trains down, but for country dances and at all other times they looped them up to the left. Perhaps the explanation is that for the formal minuet the train was unlooped but held, as the train worn down was an indication of Royal status.

The mantua was not the only form of dress worn to Court. The sack or *sacque* was, like the mantua, originally a loose dress. When accepted as a court style in the 1770's and 1780's it was however fitted more closely to the body. It was certainly worn by certain members of the Royal Household, as appropriate to their station. The

COURT DRESS WITH THE NEW HOOP
INVENTED BY MRS BELL, 52 ST JAMES'S
Fashion plate published in *La Belle
Assemblée* June 1817. The white dress
is trimmed with garlands of pink
roses.

actress Sarah Siddons at the time a member of
the Household, had to wear hers, and when
called to read to the King and Queen 'one could
not appear in the presence of the Queen except
in a dress called a *sacque*'. A remark made by
Sophie von La Roche suggests that the sack was
worn by others. She is clear that the dress she
helped Countess Reventlow into was a sack.

A survey of ladies' court dress styles would
be incomplete without some attempt to analyse
the function of the *corps de robe*. Mrs Delany saw
this 'stiff bodied gown' worn by the bride and
her attendants at the marriage of the Princess
Royal with the Prince of Orange. The *corps de
robe* was on this occasion worn with a train that
was borne by eight peers' daughters. These
bridesmaids wore similar gowns as the Royal
style was extended on such an occasion. At the
Coronation of George II the Princess Royal and
her two sisters, who supported their mother's
train, were dressed in 'stiff bodied gowns of
silver tissue'. It was the *corps de robe* that the
Magazine à la Mode refers to when it describes
the Royal robe in 1777. The Queen customarily
appeared in this form of dress for formal court
functions which was 'a close body, without
pleats . . . a train descending from the waist $2\frac{1}{2}$
or 3 yards long . . . borne by a page'. In time the
Queen discarded this dress, appearing at a
Drawing Room in 1817 in a mantua and petticoat.

Royalty had a certain amount of leeway in the
way they dressed for Court, at least if the
Princess Royal is a guide. She cast off her *corps de
robe* the day after the wedding, for a mantua and
petticoat but, significantly retaining that gloss
of Royal status perhaps, her eight attendants
chose to wear their *corps de robe* to the Drawing
Room.

Although the English Court in its dress as its
manners was probably less rigid than some of its
European counterparts, there were certain
essential elements in the form of court dress that
set it apart from contemporary fashion. Principal amongst these was the hoop.

To the modern eye the structured nature of
court dress is not particularly surprising as
women have been confined by understructures
in their clothes for several hundred years. The
skirt of the eighteenth-century court dress
however presents alterations, of considerable
scale, to the basic female form. The fantastic

exaggeration of the lower part of the dress was achieved by wearing whalebone hoops. Coming into fashionable wear in about 1710 the hoop (in various forms) remained a part of full dress until about 1780. It was retained for court wear for forty years thereafter. The shape and scale of the court hoop was one of the hallmarks of English court dress from the 1730's. Swift had seen an early example of the hoop in 1711 and did not approve. He wrote to his ladies in Ireland: 'Have you got the whalebone petticoats amongst you yet? I hate them; a woman may hide a moderate gallant under them.'

On the other hand it was a 'delightful moment' for Sophie von La Roche when she offered her hand to the Countess 'for her to step into her hoop to which the skirt was already attached', in 1786. The *Belle Assemblée* was showing hooped dresses for the English Court, but also the more fashionable line without hoops, for the French Court, in 1817. Perhaps this fossilization of fashion in England in the early nineteenth century had something to do

with the fact that the country had not undergone the traumatic experience of revolution in the same way that France had, when social and political upheaval swept away the Royal Court along with its traditions and apparel.

During the eighteenth century the hoop did not remain unchanged in form. Mrs Delany, describing the hoops worn by her contemporaries in 1756, says that 'Hoops are as flat as if made of pasteboard and as stiff, sloping from the hip and spreading at the bottom, enormous.' This was called a French hoop and was considered an improvement, as it was not 'so ugly as the square hoops, known as the English hoops'. By the 1790's the fashionable neo-classical style of dress with a raised waistline favoured a bell-shaped hoop. Marcus writing in *La Belle Assemblée* in 1819 says these were uncouth. It certainly presented the wearer with severe practical problems. Riding to Court in her sedan chair which she entered and left with difficulty 'the wearer banged backwards and forwards in

A LADY IN FULL DRESS FOR THE DRAWING ROOM IN JANUARY 1777. Fashion plate published in *Magazine à la Mode*.

Heideloff's Gallery of Fashion Fashion
plate July 1796.

HER ROYAL HIGHNESS, THE PRINCESS OF
WALES IN HER COURT DRESS ON JUNE 4
1807 AS AUTHENTICALLY TAKEN FROM
THE REAL DRESS MADE BY MRS WEBB OF
PALL MALL. Fashion illustration
published in *La Belle Assemblée* July
1807.

A LADY IN A COURT DRESS
Fashion plate published by Tabart and
Company June 4 1805.

Heideloff's Gallery of Fashion Fashion
plate July 1794.

Heideloff's Gallery of Fashion Fashion plate February 1796. The petticoat is of white satin trimmed with heavy gold fringe, the bodice and train are of maroon and black striped velvet.

the most grotesque and ridiculous manner [and] a pair of flaming pink, silk stockings were generally very amply displayed'. How grateful therefore must the nobility have been to the inventor of the hoop publicized in 1817 which enabled the lady to sit comfortably in 'a sedan or other carriage with the same ease as [in] any other garment', since 'by this unique and un-rivalled novelty the splendour and dignity of court costume is not only preserved but con-siderably heightened'. This manner of folding the hoop was seen by Louis Simond during his tour of England: 'to enable [ladies] to sit in their sedan chairs their immense hoops are folded like wings pointing forward on each side'.

The hoop was heavy as well as inconvenient. Jane Austen's sister-in-law in 1786 writes that she wondered how she had managed to endure the Court, standing from two o'clock until four o'clock 'loaded with a great hoop of no incon-siderable weight'. Ladies were not finally to cast aside this problematical garment until 1820, when, with a new reign, ladies read that at the Drawing Room to be held on Thursday 15 June of that year the King had been pleased to dispense with hoops.

The hair was also prepared with special care. Lady Jane Coke tells her friend Mrs Eyre in

Derby in 1750 that blonde lace was usual for the head-dress at Court. The lace would have been in the form of lengths called lappets, which were pinned like streamers into the hair. Feathers too were worn and quantities of jewels added to the powdered hair completed the effect. This fashionable method of ornamenting the hair was the precursor of the feather and veil head-dress of the nineteenth and twentieth centuries. According to one historian looking back from the vantage-point of 1817, coloured powders were added to the hair to improve its natural colour and included blue, yellow and a brick dust hue. 'Great quantities of jewels' were what struck Lady Coke in 1750, and this was a feature noted by almost all of the writers of the period. For example at the Drawing Room on Thursday 26 June 1817 the Marchioness of Stafford had a head-dress of a gold tissue turban, with a helmet of feathers and a 'profusion of costly diamonds', a jewel also favoured by several other ladies present. They would also all have had fans, an essential part of the female armoury; these were often decorated with delicately painted land-scapes or allegorical scenes, but their use was not merely ornamental. Years before, Swift had described the Duchess of Shrewsbury who 'came running up to me and clapt her fan up to hide us from the company', probably while they exchanged gossip about those present.

The final effect achieved by dress, hoop, powder, jewels, lace and fan was the result of many hours of labour. Fanny Burney gives us an inkling of the time spent upon their appearance by ladies going to Court when she describes the process of getting the Queen ready. The Queen had her hair dressed at her residence at Kew Palace, before going to St James's Palace where she would put on her dress which lessened the risk of damage to the costly fabrics. Fanny had to attend from six o'clock in the morning and probably missed breakfast. Nor must the make up pot be neglected, except in the case of the young, like Georgiana later Duchess of Devonshire, whose colouring did not require rouge. Swift saw a lady he kindly declines to name without her make up 'the ugliest sight I have ever seen ... but she will soon be painted and a beauty again'.

The impression made by the jewels and the powder was reinforced by the splendour of the material from which the dress was made. Mrs Delany describes a dress the Duchess of Queensberry wore to Court 'white sattin [sic] embroidered; the bottom of the petticoat brown hills covered with all sorts of weeds and every breadth had an old stump of a tree ... round which twined nasturtiums, ivy, honey-suckles, periwinkles, convolvuluses and all sorts of twining flowers ...'.

The dresses were made from silks obtained from the mercers, middlemen who operated between the weavers and the customer. Once she knew she needed a new court dress, as Lady Coke did in January 1767, she sent to the mercer to bring her silk for her gown. In Lady Coke's case the silk alone cost £70, and she then sent to the laceman to bring some silver lace which would be used for ornament. The mantua maker would then construct the dress after the approved court style. Some ladies were cost conscious and would have existing dresses altered. Mrs Freeman is reported by Mrs Lybbe Powys to have found with relief that the mantua maker felt that there was no need to buy a new dress for Court as the style was the same as some years before, so the dress she had then worn would serve again. Lady Coke was pleased with her dress in 1767 and confides that while Lady Dalkieth's dress was fine 'I don't think so pretty

A GENTLEMAN IN COURT DRESS
Fashion plate published June 4 1805. The coat is of a dark blue material, the waistcoat white, both are decorated with embroidery in coloured silks.

41

Court suit c 1780. Cut and uncut velvet lavishly embroidered with coloured silks and sequins. The embroidery of the ivory satin waistcoat compliments that of the coat.

as my own' and she kept it for the Drawing Room following the Birthday Court at which it was originally worn.

The silk was sometimes specifically obtained from British sources. Queen Charlotte at one period specified that court gowns were to be made from silk woven in Spitalfields, in what is now the East End of London, while in 1745 there was a campaign to relieve the suffering of the Irish weavers, whose trade was depressed, by appearing in a variety of 'Irish stuffs'. On this occasion, according to Mrs Delany, while the ladies supported the worthy cause, many of the gentlemen did not as their suits were made from foreign materials.

Discussion of gentlemen's court dress during the eighteenth century is handicapped by the fact that it is only on rare occasions that the writers who enthused about ladies dress spared a thought about what their escorts wore. Indeed Mrs Delany confesses in 1734 that 'I hardly remember men's clothes'. Perhaps she ran out of adjectives, or simply did not have space in her letters.

This is a great pity since there are few visual references to fall back upon. The traditions of English portraiture, favouring a more informal style of dress rarely depict subjects in court suits. A notable exception to this rule is the portrait of an unknown man about 1713 by A. S. Belle, showing the subject in a court suit of light brown silk, the waistcoat decorated with a design of foliage worked in gold. The style of the suit—coat, waistcoat and breeches, with the waistcoat in a different but usually complementary pattern—was to remain constant through most of the period. The lines of the suit changed with the prevailing fashion, so that in about 1700 a tall, slim silhouette was favoured, changing in the 1720's as the skirts of the coat flared out, with stiffened pleats. From the 1750's onwards the line again became more slender, the pleats moved to the back, the waistcoat shortened.

When Mrs Delany can recall what the gentlemen wore, the descriptions strike the modern reader as no less remarkable than the clothing of the ladies, despite her qualification in 1738 that there was 'nothing extraordinary among the men'. There was (of course) 'much finery' and this was chiefly manifested in suits of luxury fabrics ornamented with gold or silver embroid-

Court suit c 1795. Blue and black spotted silk embroidered in coloured silks, probably French.

ery and 'rich waistcoats'. Lord Baltimore was in 'light brown and silver'. Silks and velvets were usual materials, Lord Essex in 1722 in a waistcoat of pink lutestring, a glossy silk fabric. Sarah Osborne considered the pink Padua soie coats of several other men rather unmanly. The Duke of Portland was 'very fine' in 1753 in dark mouse-coloured velvet embroidered with silver, Mr Hanger wearing for the Queen's Birthday in 1776 'sky blue Padua soie, the seams worked with gold, cuffs and waistcoat'. Mr Hanger's display did not, according to Mrs Lybbe Powys, end with the suit, for he carried a velvet muff trimmed with lace and wore a large white feather in his hat.

As one would expect the Royal Family dressed with particular splendour. Even the ill-favoured Prince of Orange wore to his wedding and at the Court the following day 'a gold stuff embroidered with silver . . . rich but not showy', while the King, also in gold stuff had diamond buttons to his coat.

But during the closing years of the eighteenth century, movements in society dictated a less ostentatious fashion for gentlemen's court suits. Much plainer fabrics were used from about 1820 bringing about the final eclipse of the peacock male. His place was taken by a creature who wore a court suit of similar cut, but now of a woollen facecloth, of subdued colour, the waistcoat the last opportunity for display, made of white or cream silk embroidered with coloured silks, in a floral pattern. Embroidery had been banished from the coat after lingering for a few years down the front and around the pockets.

Two fossilized elements remained in the gentlemen's appearance when at court. The two-cornered hat or *chapeau bras*, usually carried, and the sword. Swords were retained for court wear after they had been discarded from fashionable civilian dress in about 1775. The style that was worn was the 'court' or 'small sword', a weapon designed for thrusting with a slim, tapered and sometimes fluted blade, a guard with a loop to protect the knuckles and sometimes a shell or pair of shells at the base of the hilt. Hilts were of silver and silver gilt, decorated with diamonds, or faceted steel cut to resemble the precious stone, which was a fashion particularly favoured in England. Diamonds incidentally were often worn on buckles. In 1756 the Hon John Spencer going to pay court to the Prince of Wales had

COURT DRESS. QUEEN'S BIRTHDAY
JANUARY 18 1799.
Fashion plate published in *Fashions of
London and Paris*. The white dress is
patterned in mauve and gold. The
lines, tassels and other trimmings are
gold.

diamond buckles on his shoes worth, according
to one observer, £30,000.

As dress at Court was affected by Royal
Birthdays and Weddings, so the demise of a
member of the Royal Family triggered off a
flurry of changes as the Court went into carefully regulated periods of mourning for which
certain colours would be worn. Black crape and
bombazine were always in demand upon such
occasions, and when George II died in 1760 one
shop was reported as having sold 1500 yards of
black material in one night. Black ribbons
would be worn, which could decorate dress of
different although strictly regulated colours. On
the death of Princess Louisa in 1768, Lady Mary
Coke says that the order was for white and silver
with black ribbon. Black could be worn too, but
not white alone. At times during the mourning
this would change. Lady Shelbourne appeared
at the Drawing Room in white and silver as she
thought correct but was sent home to change,
while on another occasion even the Royal Maids
of Honour got it wrong, coming to Chapel in
dresses of white lutestring and being sent back
to change into white with silver.

White was a traditional colour for mourning,
dating as far back as Imperial Rome and used in
Spain until the fifteenth century, perhaps as
symbolic of hope of the life to come. In 1781 the
Lord Chamberlain's Office commanded ladies
coming to Court to wear white or white and
gold or white and silver as alternative to black,
although black ribbons were to be worn. Gentlemen too could appear in plain white suits or
white with silver or gold waistcoats. The hilts of
their swords and their buckles would also be
coloured. In half mourning and in a less formal
order of dress grey was permitted, as for example in the early decades of the nineteenth
century when grey silk dresses for ladies and
grey frocks (a type of undress coat) for men
were acceptable. One colour was however the
exclusive preserve of Royalty during mourning
and this was purple. Cesar de Sassure noted
King George II in a purple cloth suit with knots
of black crape for court mourning, with a silver
waistcoat.

The duration of court mourning depended
upon the importance to the Court of the de-
ceased Royal. For example Queen Caroline,
consort of George II had her death marked by
six months of mourning. Louise, daughter of

the Grand Duke of Saxe Weimar and consort of the Hereditary Grand Duke of Mecklenburgh Schwerin was a more distant connection of the English throne and when she died in 1816 the Court was in mourning for only seven days. For the initial period of deep mourning, which lasted from 22–25 February ladies dresses had to be of silk or linen but from 25 February until the end of the period silk or velvet was allowed and white with silver or gold material could be worn.

When the Court came out of mourning, some ladies were caught unawares. In 1820 a period of court mourning came unexpectedly to an end and even the Royal princesses, according to Fanny Burney, had had half mourning dresses of white and black made, which were consequently wasted. There seems to have been a sigh of relief when normal court wear could be resumed. Richard Rush, recording his experiences of the English Court under the Regency, remarks that the occasion of the first

Drawing Room following the end of mourning for Princess Charlotte, only daughter of the Prince Regent and Caroline of Brunswick, was like 'the bursting out of Spring'.

For two valedictory views of ladies at the Georgian Court, which taken together provide a truer image of these fantastical creatures than either in isolation, we might do worse than record the words of Louis Simond and Richard Rush. Simond, no friend of the hoop, had a less than reverential opinion of the ladies, no longer in the first flush of youth whom he spied in their sedan chairs on their way to the Drawing Room. 'That face, painted up to the eyes ... and the glasses of the vehicle drawn up that the winds of heaven may not visit the powder and paint too roughly ... and this piece of natural history thus cased does not ill resemble the foetus of a hippopotamus in a brandy bottle.'

Contrast this with Richard Rush, Minister to the Court of St James's from the United States. Considering the ladies at the Queen's Drawing

Heideloff's Gallery of Fashion Detail of fashion plate February 1801. A bright pink bodice accompanies a white petticoat edged in pink and trimmed with gold. Pink and white feathers surmount the golden diadem head-dress.

Room in 1818 he says that 'they appeared like beautiful architecture the hoops the base the plume the pinnacle. Like old English buildings and Shakespeare ... it triumphed over criticism'.

Heideloff's Gallery of Fashion Fashion plate July 1797.

COURT DRESSES FOR HER MAJESTY'S BIRTHDAY. Fashion plate published in *Le Beau Monde* 1807.

47

CHAPTER THREE

Manners and Rules

Court Dress 1820–1900

Richard Rush considered the Drawing Room which he attended in February 1818 would have served as a good model for the Court of the period. 'The hoop dresses of the ladies, sparkling with lamé their plumes; their lappets; the various costumes of the gentlemen.' A painter might have used the scene to illustrate the Court under the Prince Regent.

A painter commissioned to epitomize the late Victorian Court eighty years later would have shown different styles of dress, but his picture would have captured the same spirit. Throughout the nineteenth century the Court was remarkable above all in the way in which during a period of extraordinary economic, political and social change it remained essentially unaltered in its attitudes and in the codes which governed its behaviour. A courtier transported from the Drawing Room of Queen Charlotte to that of her grand-daughter would soon have felt at home and his clothes would not have struck anyone present as particularly old-fashioned.

Ladies' dress did change, following the line of fashion and there were developments in the way in which news of the Court was communicated to the world, magazines such as *The Queen* becoming a valuable source of information on who was presented and what was worn. Yet the image the Court had of itself and the degree of exclusiveness it attempted to impose upon its proceedings did not move with the times. The reigns of George IV, William IV and Victoria are replete with reminders to ladies and gentlemen attending Court of standards below which they must not fall. In 1834 the Lord Chamberlain's Office had to point out that some ladies had taken to appearing at Queen Adelaide's Drawing Room in hats, feathers and turbans. This was contrary to etiquette and all ladies were to

wear feathers and lappets. Nearly fifty years later Lord Hartford, Queen Victoria's Lord Chamberlain, gave out a similar notice: ladies attending the Drawing Room must appear in feather head-dresses and white lappets (or, a concession to modernity, veils). Coloured feathers were contrary to regulation. The Court, not the rest of the world, decided how the Court would change, if at all.

This increasing conservatism of attitudes was due in part to the fact that the Court was no longer a part of the political life of the nation, in the sense that it had been in the eighteenth century. The reform of the electoral system and the creation of the party system of politics had led to a slow separation of the monarch, and the Court from the centre of political power and influence. After the reforms of the Royal Household, which occurred at the end of the eighteenth and in the early nineteenth century there were fewer lucrative posts in the gift of the officers of the Court. All three monarchs after 1821 cultivated this conservatism in respect of court life, which had the effect of isolating it from society at large. For George IV to adopt the role of guardian of standards of dress and behaviour is not surprising given that monarch's obsession with clothes and appearance. Like his brother, William IV, and niece, Victoria, George had an extensive knowledge of the minutiae of correct dress, and a sharp eye open for falling standards. Captain Gronow recalled in his *Reminiscences* that having got used to the new fashion for wearing trousers while in Paris, he wore a pair in the Prince Regent's presence, and was reminded that the style was not acceptable in England.

It is no surprise to find George IV tightened up the regulations governing presentations at

THE STAIRCASE AT BUCKINGHAM PALACE. Engraving published in *The Graphic*
March 1870 showing ladies and gentlemen congregating before a Drawing
Room.

COURT DRESS OF LADY WORSLEY
HOLMES AT THE FIRST DRAWING ROOM
OF GEORGE IV INVENTED BY MRS BELL,
52 ST JAMES'S STREET. Published in *La
Belle Assemblée* August 1820.

Facing page. COURT DRESS Fashion plate
1831. The lady wears a short veil in
place of lace lappets.

Court. On 1 May 1824 the Lord Chamberlain's
Office published a set of regulations to be
observed at Court. Ladies who proposed to
attend the Drawing Room to be held on 13 May
had to take with them two cards, each engraved
with their name. One of these cards was to be
left with the page in the Presence Chamber, and
the other given to the Lord in Waiting who
would announce the lady to the King. In addition the lady had previously to have obtained
the name of a sponsor who could vouch for her
suitability for presentation at court, and this
sponsor's name had had to be submitted to the
King some days before the presentation.

There were further adjustments to the system, introduced by William IV. There could be
no greater contrast between two monarchs and
brothers than George IV and William IV.
George, ostentatious, a lover of ceremony and
William a career sailor who had spent most of
his life away from Court. George IV had spent
about £250,000 on his coronation whereas William had initially not wanted a coronation at all.
He made the point to his advisors that as he was
an old man and therefore unlikely to be on the
throne for long it would be a waste of money.
He would have been content to be taken to
Parliament before his coronation in a hackney
carriage. When his courtiers were in the midst
of debating whether he should wear a crown for
the occasion or not, he seized the crown and
placing it on his head announced that the coronation had taken place. In the event the actual
coronation cost only £30,000, and in memory of
George IV's extravagant affair became known by
contrast as the 'half crown ation'. William and
Adelaide's Court was considered dull and the
King's informality disconcerting to those who
remembered his brother. Yet despite the difference in style the process of regulating the
formality of the Court was in no way to be held
back under William. His brother had insisted
upon ladies bringing with them two cards to
Court: William required three, one for the page
in the Presence Chamber, one for the Lord in
Waiting and one for the Lord Chamberlain who
would henceforth announce the name of the
lady to Queen Adelaide. There were regulations
too which spelt out exactly how one was to
behave. The person to be presented was to kneel
on the right knee, kiss the King's hand, rise,
bow and leave the room.

A DRAWING ROOM HELD BY QUEEN VICTORIA AND PRINCE ALBERT
Watercolour attributed to Henry Barraud showing ladies being presented to
Queen Victoria and Prince Albert.

As more and more rules were announced, commercial publications began to appear, to advise on correct procedures. One of these was the *Court and Country Companion*, published in 1835. In addition to giving orders of social precedence, lessons on how to write to various ranks of person, this publication gave detailed instructions on what you were to do at a Court presentation, Levee, Drawing Room or Birthday Court. Finding a sponsor was an essential first step, but as important was the knowledge of how to conduct oneself. The presentee is taken carefully through the various stages of the ritual. Advice is even given on what should be done if one's own carriage and servants were not for some reason available—a livery stable will hire out the 'handsom chariot, with respectable coachman and footman'. In a hired or one's own carriage you arrive at St James's Palace for a levee, two cards clutched in a gloved hand—a further one having a day or so before been presented to the Lord Chamberlain's Office. First, one walks to the Presence Chamber and then directed by the page, to whom one card is delivered, into the Audience Chamber. Here gloves are removed, the hat is

taken in the left hand and the remaining card given to the Lord in Waiting who, at the levee, would announce you. When presented a gentleman kneels on one knee (the right) kisses the royal hand, rises, bows and backs away.

The Court and Country Companion, and other similar publications were answering a need: more people than ever before felt themselves entitled to be presented at Court. As a consequence there was a ready market for information about the Court, its protocol and character, which is almost invariably described as brilliant and fascinating. The same publication comes to the conclusion that a British Drawing Room is the most fascinating of any in Europe. Over half a century later the *Lady's Pictorial* pronounced the Drawing Room held by Queen Victoria in May 1895 to be 'the most successful of the season ... the gowns and jewels and the flowers were all of the loveliest description possible'.

Nevertheless not everyone was to be admitted. Lady Violet Greville, writing in *The Gentlewoman in Society*, noted with poorly concealed contempt that 'rich merchants, people in business ... American cousins' now wanted to be presented, and that there were too few restrictions applied to the process. Restrictions however there were. *Rules and Manners of Good Society* listed the type of person who would be eligible for presentation at Court, including members of the aristocracy, members of the cabinet, officers in the armed forces, but is clear that at 'trade known as retail trade the line is drawn absolutely'. Sponsors would have to vouch for unblemished character if required, and although as a rule divorce was a bar to presentation, Queen Victoria did allow ladies who were the innocent parties in divorce cases to appear at Court, as she records in her journal in May 1887.

Apart from this attempt to accommodate in some small way contemporary manners, Victoria's Court was as strictly regulated as those of her uncles, William and George IV.

The London Gazette for 14 July 1837, less than a month after the Queen's accession to the throne, set the tone for the following sixty-four years. It repeated the requirements for the numbers of cards to be presented and the importance of a sponsor. The function of the Drawing Room was the culmination of the process of 'coming out'. Everyone present had a part to play even if it was only to provide appropriate background decoration. *Letters to a Bride*, which included *Letters to a Debutante* by L H Armstrong published in 1894, described the progress of a young lady through the ritual. When she arrived at Buckingham Palace she would cross the Great Hall and make her way up the Grand Staircase to meet a page to whom she would present her first card, then pass into the first saloon and then through a succession of rooms until reaching the Throne Room she,

THE QUEEN'S DRAWING ROOM. THE AMBASSADORS ENTRANCE BUCKINGHAM PALACE. AUGUST 1868. An engraving. Foreign diplomats and their ladies were granted the privilege known as the *entrée*, which permitted use of this special entrance.

QUEEN ADELAIDE'S FIRST DRAWING ROOM OF 1834. Watercolour by Théodore Leblanc. The Drawing Room depicted took place on 24 February. The young Princess Victoria attended with her mother.

Miss Lloyd in court dress c 1865.
Photograph by Camille Silvy. The
dress conforms in all respects to the
guidelines discussed in contemporary
journals.

along with other debutantes, would be presented. Quickly passing through the room reserved for the *Corps Diplomatique* there was a
brief rest to 'recover yourself a little and chat
over the events with your friends'. The ordeal
of the day was not over, however, for after
leaving the Palace you would give or attend a
Drawing Room tea at which the day's events
and the clothes that had graced or disgraced
them would be discussed.

It was, in the words of Lady Violet Greville,
writing in the *Gentlewoman in Society*, 'a serious
matter to choose a Drawing Room Dress'. The
dress for ladies attending Court during the
period 1820 to 1900 was determined by the
fashionable line of evening dress, and the regulations laid down by the Lord Chamberlain's
Office. Female fashion during these years
moved away from the tubular high waisted look
of the early nineteenth century, the waist
becoming lower and tighter and the skirt fuller
from about 1825. The shape of the skirt was
initially achieved by layers of petticoats which
were starched, but in about 1856 the artificial
cage crinoline was invented, a structure of
whalebone, wire or watch spring which supported the skirt. From the late 1860s the front of
the skirt began to flatten and the emphasis move
to the rear, the bodice remaining tightly cor-
seted. During 1870 the full bustle style arrived,
the rear supported again by a wire or horsehair
structure. By 1890 the skirt was evolving towards the 'S' shape associated with the Edwar-
dian period.

Court dress followed these developments but,
although the Drawing Rooms were held in the
afternoon, society ladies were still expected to
wear low cut evening bodices for day attendance at Court. The low cut bodice was not
always accepted with enthusiasm. *The Queen* for
23 March 1867, revealed one reason for this. It
reported 'the poor belles at the court on Tues-
day seemed to suffer a great deal from excessive
cold'. It was never a pleasure to wear a low dress
in broad daylight 'and when the snow is falling
hard and fast and the temperature is below
freezing point it is a trial indeed'.

The dresses were as splendid as those of
mothers and grandmothers who had attended
earlier Courts. Countess Howe wore to Queen
Adelaide's Drawing Room in 1834 a dress of
white satin and silver, the bodice ornamented

with blonde lace and diamonds, and the head-dress of ostrich feathers with lappets of blonde lace and diamonds. Sixty years later the Countess Templeton was resplendent in ivory satin, embroidered with silver, with a train suspended from one shoulder of coral moiré brocade lined with ivory satin and caught up with artificial carnations. What distinguished these dresses from the full evening dress of their respective contemporaries were the additions of head-dress and train, and we must look at the way in which these developed over the years to see how the Lord Chamberlain's Office became the regulating body dictating the dress of ladies at Court.

There were at the beginning of this period rumours that the hoop was to be revived. *The Ladies Cabinet*, in December 1838, reported this as a matter of certainty, but if whispers to this effect had been heard they were not translated into action: the Lord Chamberlain's Office in St James's Palace at the command of the Queen would have had to order ladies into hoops once more. Queen Victoria seems an unlikely monarch to have thought seriously about reviving memories of the Courts of her Hanoverian ancestors. But it is interesting to note that *The Ladies Cabinet* considered the train as an essential partner to the hoop, the one balancing the effect of the other.

It was during the nineteenth century that the train became a sign of the most formal order of court dress. Its length increased from about four feet from the ankles in 1840, to eight feet in the 1870s and even longer by the end of the century. Indeed Lady Cambell remarked in 1893 that 'the train is of great length and breadth . . . it is made of a more costly and handsome material than the other parts of the dress [and] velvet or satin is chosen and it is trimmed with lace and feathers or flowers to correspond [to the dress]'.

Until about 1870 it was important that the train be fastened only from the waist. *The Queen* reported in 1867 that amongst the rules governing ladies' court dress were those affecting the trains. They must hang from the waist and not from the shoulders. One lady felt this was inelegant and so had two wide strips of material made up from the same material as the train and put these on the shoulders so that it appeared the train was fastened at this level. By the 1890s trains could be fastened asymmetrically—from the shoulder or waist, or from both. The *Lady's*

Mrs Aspinall in court dress c 1865. Photograph by Camille Silvy. Mrs Aspinall's dress demonstrates the large scale and elaborate nature of court dresses of this decade.

Pictorial of May 1894 reports the train of the Countess of Antrim fastened from both shoulders, that of the Marchioness of Hertford, (in dark petunia velvet edged with yellow), attached partly from the shoulder and partly from the waist, while the Lady Hughes had a train that hung from both shoulders but was 'gracefully caught a little below the waist'. The Hon Mrs Russel wore a train of pale blue duchesse satin hanging from one shoulder, whereas the Duchess of Cleveland clung to the older style and wore her black satin and white *faille* stripe silk, lined and edged with white satin, trimmed with rows of black spangles, from the waist.

There was a skill in transporting the considerable bulk of velvet and silk, hung from shoulder or waist. During the early part of the Drawing Room, before the actual Presentation, the train was carried on the left arm, folded carefully in a large box pleat. As one entered the Presence Chamber a Royal Page took the train and spread it on the ground. After her deep curtsey to the Queen and other members of the Royal Family present, the lady would back out of the Chamber, and would therefore have to rely on her own training and the sense of timing of the Page to pick up the train and pass it over her arm once more.

Less cumbersome than what she wore from her shoulders or waist, but equally important in the livery of the debutante was the head-dress. *Letters to a Bride* points out that it is 'compulsory for both married and unmarried ladies to wear plumes'. With these would be worn lappets or veils of silk tulle. *The Queen* in 1869 describing the head-dress worn to Court said that 'they generally consist of two small feathers worn on the top of the head'. A few at this date retained the older fashion of one large feather and one smaller one. Ladies from time to time tried to relax the rules about head-dresses. The Lord

Chamberlain's Office during William IV's reign reminded them that they were to appear at Drawing Rooms in feathers and lappets and not in turbans. During Queen Victoria's reign there was a time when unmarried ladies wore two and married ladies three feathers.

With dress, train and feathers, long white kid gloves, bouquets or fans were the costume for full court dress. There were however occasions when even in the presence of royalty, one or other of these elements would be discarded, as indication that a lesser degree of formality was required, or a particular ceremony was being celebrated. For example at State Balls trains and plumes were not always appropriate. In 1842 the Lord Chamberlain's Office directed the ladies who were to attend the Queen's Ball on 12 May not to appear in trains or plumes. In the same year when the Court was at the Palace of Holyroodhouse in Edinburgh ladies who were received by the Queen were not required to

COURT DRESS. Detail of fashion plate published in *Ackermann's Repository of Arts* 1822.

FASHIONABLE COURT DRESS FOR MAY 1826 INVENTED BY MISS PIERPOINT, EDWARD STREET, PORTMAN SQUARE. Detail of fashion plate published in the *Lady's Monthly Magazine*.

wear trains or plumes. Nor at Royal Weddings were trains always worn by the general company. For example at Queen Victoria's wedding to Prince Albert in 1840 full court dress *without trains* was specified for some guests, while for the Prince of Wales' marriage with Princess Alexandra, the *London Gazette* recorded that the ladies in the general company invited to the Chapel Royal wore full dress, without trains, but with plumes. At both the weddings of the Princess Royal in 1858 and Princess Helena in 1866 trains were not generally worn. Special instructions had to be issued for the marriage from Osborne House on the Isle of Wight between Princess Beatrice and Prince Henry of Battenbergh: ladies who were staying on the island wore long dresses and their hair arranged as for evening, while those who travelled to the island for the day only were allowed to wear bonnets and morning dresses.

Clearly then while dresses, trains and feathers together made up the costume for Drawing Rooms and the presentations that took place at them, they were only elements in a system of dress to be worn or not as the occasion demanded.

Royal weddings were not the only time when this was so. At the coronation of George IV court dresses with plumes but without lappets or trains were worn and at the first Drawing

COURT TRAINS DESIGNED IN PARIS FOR THE FORTHCOMING DRAWING ROOMS
Fashion plate published in *The Queen* 1888.

THE DRAWING ROOM HELD BY HRH THE PRINCESS OF WALES ON BEHALF OF THE
QUEEN AT BUCKINGHAM PALACE April 23 1896. Drawing by S Begg.

Room following the coronation of William IV
and Adelaide all peers and peeresses were
obliged to wear their coronation robes and
coronets. As in the eighteenth century death,
like weddings and coronations, influenced court
dress. Queen Victoria seems always to have had
a deep interest in mourning—on the death of
the Tsar of Russia during the Crimean War she
had her officials scour the records to discover
the correct procedure for court mourning for a
monarch with whose country one happened at
the time to be at war.

In a sense the Court never went out of
mourning for Prince Albert. Between 16
December 1861 and the end of the year, in the
immediate aftermath of his death, court mourning was at its deepest: ladies had to wear dresses
of black wool trimmed with crape, plain linen,
black shoes, gloves and crape fans. From 1
January black silk was permitted, but feathers

had to be black, and everyone at Court remained
in mourning throughout 1862. Ladies in Waiting continued to wear black thereafter. Maids of
Honour, in deference to their youth were
allowed white, grey, mauve or purple, and
servants at Windsor had to wear an armband of
black crape for eight years.

Lesser degrees of mourning required other
combinations of colour. For a week in March
1869 the Queen ordered mourning for the Duke
of Schleswig Holstein Senderburg Augusten-
berg, her second cousin and father of one of her
sons-in-law. Black dresses were ordered, with
white gloves, black and white shoes, feathers
and fans, pearls, diamonds or ornaments of
plain gold or silver.

By the end of the nineteenth century it had
become a convention that a debutante's dress
should be white. This had not always been the
case, as the *Belle Assembleé* makes clear by

Court dress c 1875. Cream silk with double-faced satin stripe in purple and yellow, trimmed with blonde lace.

COSTUME DE LA COUR D'ANGLETERRE
Fashion plate published in *Revue de la Mode* c 1860.

implication when it remarks in 1807 that *several* 'young and lovely women' wore white to a Drawing Room. By the 1860s references are being made to a white dress being appropriate for the debutante. One worried husband whose wife was to be presented in 1867 wrote to the Lord Chamberlain's Office to enquire if the popular idea that all ladies being presented had to wear white was correct, since if it applied only to the debutante, and not the married lady, his wife would not require a new dress for the occasion. In the event she would probably not have felt out of place in a coloured dress, since *The Queen* in 1869 makes it clear that only 'young girls' who were to be presented should 'appear in white, white tulle, white crape or white net skirts, worn over silk, satin or moiré petticoats to match, with silk, satin or moiré trains'. Pearls were the recommended jewels, or silver jewellery, and bouquets of lilies of the valley, white may or myrtle were to be carried. The lappets of their grandmothers and mothers were less popular than veils of white tulle.

Once a lady had been presented she would

expect to repeat the ordeal following marriage, as she had now joined a new family—that of her husband, and would be presented by her mother-in-law. On this occasion the wedding dress would usually be worn. This was often white, although *Letters to a Bride*, in 1896, says that 'If you prefer a little colour it is not against the rules (on presentation after marriage).' A 'suspicion' of pink in the material of the dress, pink lining to the train, and a bouquet of half blown pink roses could be introduced into the costume.

Some wedding dresses that have been worn to presentations at Court have survived. They reveal that the high-necked wedding gown, and its sleeves, had to be altered to conform with the regulations of court dress. Some ingenious dressmakers incorporated detachable sleeves, which could be removed by unfastening hooks and eyes, the bodice turned down to the appropriate line of *décolletage*.

Royalty were not exempt from the regulations that were applied to the Queen's other subjects. Princess Mary of Teck, daughter of the

Lady Charlotte Innes Kerr in court
dress c 1865. Photograph by Camille
Silvy. Lady Charlotte's black ostrich
feather head-dress, veil and gloves
indicate deep mourning.

Mrs Alexander Kelso Hamilton in
court dress c 1890. Photograph by
Bassano. Mrs Hamilton presented her
daughter Miss Geraldine Hamilton on
this occasion.

Photograph of an unknown debutante
c 1875. This is a classic example of a
fashionable studio photograph of a
lady in court dress, carrying a feather
trimmed fan.

'THE HAUNTED LADY OR THE GHOST IN THE LOOKING GLASS' Engraving published in *Punch* July 1863. A lady in elaborate evening dress is shown admiring herself in the looking glass. She sees not only her own reflection but also the figure of the weary dressmaker.

Duke and Duchess of Teck, and future wife of George v was presented at a Drawing Room in March 1886. Her gown was of white satin, with a veil of pearl dotted tulle, the bodice of the dress draped with the same material edged with satin. She wore a diamond necklace and carried a bouquet of white roses, gardenias and lilies of the valley.

Princess Mary might have had her dress made by one of the court dressmakers who plied their business from 'houses' in the West End of London. Beneath these roofs were united the trades of milliner and dressmaker.

Charles Worth may be thought of as the first couturier in the modern sense of the word. Trained as a textile retailer he conceived of a system whereby he would show a customer a design in a number of fabrics, which he could supply along with the expertise to make up the dress. The Court was important to Worth—in fact he achieved his breakthrough in Paris by securing the patronage of Pauline von Metternich, wife of the Austrian Ambassador to the Court of Napoleon III. For much of the latter half of the nineteenth century, both in France and England, Worth was a dictator of fashion. The introduction of the Princess line in the late 1860s is attributed to him, named after the

Court dress c 1850. Worn by the Duchess of Kent (Queen Victoria's mother), the dress is made of silver tissue brocaded with floral sprays in coloured silks trimmed with silver lace.

HER MAJESTY'S DRAWING ROOM AT BUCKINGHAM PALACE—WAITING TO BE PRESENTED. Drawing by Arthur Hopkins. The ladies' trains are arranged on the floor before they enter the Throne Room.

Princess of Wales. Other couturiers were Paquin and James Redfern. The latter began as a draper on the Isle of Wight and rose to be appointed to both Queen Victoria and the Princess of Wales. His business was in Bond Street.

When dressmaking businesses first opened in the West End, contemporaries were surprised at the elegant accommodation which was commonly thought more appropriate as the town house of a member of the aristocracy than a place of business. The convenience of patronizing such an establishment was clear. Having secured an invitation to a Drawing Room a lady would be taken in her carriage to the 'house' and met at the front door by a footman. In the showroom she would be looked after by a saleswoman, usually known as a '*magasinière*', who showed styles and materials from which to choose. After the customer left the saleswoman passed the order to the 'first hand' dressmaker. It was this woman who might call upon the customer to take measurements, often arriving in a carriage, with a liveried footman belonging to the 'house' she worked for. The image presented was of unhurried elegance and service, which could nevertheless be relied upon to deliver the finished goods at a competitive price and on time.

But the conditions under which such elegance and efficiency was achieved were appalling. In the same building as the showroom, women worked long hours at low rates of pay to produce competitively priced court gowns in the limited time dictated by the client.

The economics of the court and couture trade were relatively simple. There was a demand, concentrated, for court dresses during the few months of the season. There was no monopoly

68

Arthur Hopkins

and there was a plentiful supply of cheap labour—either from young girls from the country, or those whose impecunious circumstances obliged them to earn a living.

There was a major exposé of working conditions, after the death of Mary Anne Walkeley in June 1863. Aged 20, at the time of her demise, she was employed with Madame Elise, a court dressmaker whose business was at 170 Regent Street. The inquest found that she died of apoplexy. *The Englishwoman's Domestic Magazine*, declared that it was not due to 'the apoplexy of high living' but was due to the appalling conditions in which she lived and worked. She shared a small room and bed with another employee—'herself too tired and listless to observe how deep was her companion's sleep, had probably lain by the side of a corpse all night'. She would have collapsed into this bed having worked a

typical day at a court dressmakers during the Season. *The Queen* in January 1869 reported that 'we have been told girls have been employed . . . from five in the morning of one day till one or two in that of the next, kept awake with strong tea and coffee'. For her labours she earned between £4 and £20 a year in addition to board and lodging depending upon skill and seniority.

The scandal of Miss Walkeley's death led to a commission of inquiry and the exposure of the conditions to the public. *Punch* even produced a cartoon 'the Ghost in the Looking Glass' in June 1864 in which a saleswoman stands by a young lady who is wearing her new gown and looking at herself in a mirror. She sees not only her reflection, but also that of the corpse of the dressmaker who has sewn her dress. *The Englishwoman's Domestic Magazine*, having reviewed the state of the trade, had a message for its readers.

69

Mr Walkinshaw in court dress c 1865.
Photograph by Camille Silvy.
Walkinshaw wears a cloth suit with
cut steel buttons and an embroidered
silk waistcoat, a legacy of early 19th
century fashionable styles for
gentlemen.

Court suit. Mulberry cloth with
embroidered silk waistcoat, worn by
Edward Bowra, official of the Chinese
Customs House to the English Court
1866. Bowra accompanied Pin Ch'un,
Hon Permanent Under Secretary and
Legate to Prince Kung, President of
the Tsungli Yamen.

'Ladies, there is no disguising the fact, have
been much to blame . . . economy in the service
of getting finery cheap means really the most
heartless expenditure . . . the expenditure of the
lives of their poor sisters.'

As an example, albeit an extreme one, of the
interrelation of social etiquette and economics,
the court dressmaking trade could hardly be
bettered in the nineteenth century. *Punch*, during the period a frequent critic of the whole
process of Drawing Rooms, and Presentations,
proclaimed in 1848 that 'It is well known that
for the good of trade chiefly if not entirely
the Queen holds her Levees and Drawing
rooms . . .'.

The same article continues with a diatribe
against the costume in which gentlemen were
expected to appear at court. It asks why they
were restricted to the 'footman-like costume of
the last century'. This was not comment restricted to *Punch* or the mid-century. *Etiquette of
Good Society* described the court dress of gentlemen as 'that which came to us in the days of the
early Georges, the costume of Louis Quinze'.
During the nineteenth century gentlemen's
court dress was largely determined by two
related influences: a retention of out-dated

styles, producing a distinctive form of dress, and an interest in military uniform, which by definition, places group identity and status above personality.

The first of these influences produced the court suit—a coat with tails, waistcoat and knee breeches, worn with silk stockings, and a sword with a cut steel hilt, and bicorn hat. Apart from changes in the cut of the sleeve and shoulders there was little basic alteration to these suits until the third quarter of the nineteenth century. The coat and breeches would be of fine wool cloth, or increasingly from about 1840 velvet, the waistcoat of white or cream silk, single breasted, without lapels and cut with points at the front; it would be embroidered in coloured silks in a conventional pattern of flowers. The quality of the buttons and the hilt of the sword, both of cut steel, became less fine after about 1870. A gentleman invited to the opening of the Great Exhibition in 1851 could, without fear of looking out of place, wear the court suit made for his father.

In 1869 the Lord Chamberlain's Office issued new regulations for gentlemen attending Court. A new style of suit was described in which the cloth coat and breeches were replaced with silk velvet. This had been permitted before, but in place of the embroidered waistcoat was a waistcoat of plain white silk. The cut was similar to that which had been worn before, and gilt or cut steel buttons were permitted until 1903, when the Lord Chamberlain's Office specified only the latter. Breeches were still required for the Drawing Rooms, State Balls and certain other events at Court. This regulation almost caused a diplomatic incident in 1854 when the American Ambassador, James Buchanan, interpreted the edict of his Secretary of State, that ministers of the United States when attending foreign courts were to do so in the simple dress of an American citizen, as meaning that trousers, not breeches, were to be worn. He was persuaded that a sword was appropriate, as the mark of a gentleman, but only after much delicate diplomatic

Velvet court dress (old style) 1912, illustrated in *Dress Worn at Court*. Introduced in 1869, the velvet court dress eventually replaced the cloth suit and embroidered waistcoat for gentlemen who did not have a prescribed uniform.

discussion, was Buchanan convinced that the wearing of trousers was inappropriate. He eventually appeared in black coat, white waistcoat, pantaloons and with sword.

Unlike the American Ambassador, Alfred Gilbert, the sculptor of the statue of Eros, which stands in Piccadilly Circus, was only too anxious to wear the right costume when he dined with Queen Victoria at Osborne House in 1896. Unfortunately he had not packed his breeches. His assistant, a tailor by training, managed to alter his evening dress trousers and a pair of ladies black silk stockings and a pair of court pumps were found on the Island. Meanwhile Queen Victoria, hearing of Gilbert's original difficulty, sent word that it would not be necessary to appear before her, in breeches and stockings, but the alterations were, alas, under way.

In the following chapter we shall see the full expression of the influence of uniform in court dress, as it shaped the development of special costumes for civil servants and others. So powerful was this influence, that it affected even those clothes prescribed for gentlemen who did not have a formal uniform to wear at court.

The 1869 Dress Regulations specify a levee dress of dark coloured cloth, single breasted with a stand collar, trousers of the same material and colour as the coat, both decorated with narrow gold lace, similar to that worn on certain classes of the Civil Uniform for government officials. The hat even had a gold lace loop and button similar to this uniform and the sword was to be of the same pattern. In effect therefore this was a uniform for gentlemen for whom there was no prescribed uniform. Its existence indicates the presence of a powerful urge in the Victorian male to wear uniform and to demonstrate membership of a group, perhaps seeking security and sublimating personality rather than expressing individuality, this last function today usually associated with male civilian dress.

Full court dress, including breeches, would have been worn when escorting a wife or daughter to a Drawing Room for a presentation. Unless they were performing this function men were discouraged from attending Drawing Rooms, and it is therefore to a young lady, 'Kitty', in *The Queen* of April 1867 that we turn for an account of what it was like to be presented to Queen Victoria.

Kitty wore white silk. She confessed to feeling 'dreadfully nervous' and immediately before she stepped before the Queen, wished that she had never begun the process. 'I would have given anything to have foregone the ordeal.' Her mother was already curtseying, so it was too late, and a moment later her own train was taken from her arm and arranged upon the floor by a page. She heard her name called out by the Lord Chamberlain and bent to kiss the Queen's hand. She remembered afterwards the Queen in her black dress and white veil, her ladies behind her and the uniforms of the officials. She lingered a moment and then the page was placing the train over her arm and she backed away 'as well as I was able the length of the sixty feet room and retired through a door ... sorry that this great event of my life was over'.

CHAPTER FOUR

Uniformly Splendid

The Development of Court Uniforms and Liveries

Recollecting her presentation at Court, Kitty, *The Queen*'s correspondent, wrote of the glittering uniforms of the officers of the Royal Household who stood in attendance upon Queen Victoria. The page who took her train and, after she had made her curtseys, placed it, at the correct moment, over her proferred arm, was also in a distinctive costume.

These costumes were not for everyday wear, and there were few, if any concessions to practicality: they were not for feeling relaxed in, but for fitting the individual into the impressive panorama of a Drawing Room or levee in a uniform that was at the same time both visually stunning and denied the individual any opportunity for personal ostentation. No account of the British Court would be complete therefore without a discussion of the origin and development of court liveries and uniforms.

There is a distinction to be made between these two forms of dress, although until well into the nineteenth century this was blurred. Today we are accustomed to think of livery as a special costume worn by domestic servants and uniform as a form of dress reserved for particular groups of individuals in society, such as soldiers. Armies in the Middle Ages however had clothed their members in the liveries of their lords and this tradition continued to be observed in European armies with the dress of drummers, trumpeters and other musicians wearing the livery of the regimental commander. Until the middle of the eighteenth century there was a resistance to the wearing of uniform among officers in the French and Austrian armies because it was thought to be a form of livery appropriate only to servants. The Prince de Ligne recollected that he rarely saw colonels in uniform and never generals.

It was indeed only as the idea of national armies truly took hold and the demands of supply became acute that national uniforms began to be introduced and dress regulations enforced. Gradually, although the process was to take years, the idea of uniform began to be divorced from the concept of livery.

Liveries therefore represent the earliest examples of a uniform style of costume worn at Court. It is in the accounts of the Wardrobe, the department of the Royal Household charged with organizing the supply of liveries, that we find descriptions of these clothes. Some time in the early eighteenth century an unknown official in the Lord Chamberlain's Office was set the task of establishing what footmen had worn in the Royal Household from the reign of Henry VIII onwards. Henry's footmen each had a tawney gown, edged with black velvet, a scarlet cloak, similarly decorated, two doublets, one of crimson and one of tawney and an embroidered jerkin. Under Mary I crimson velvet coats were issued and this pattern was repeated in the reigns of Elizabeth I and James I and Charles I. Probably the scarlet doublet was for full dress occasions, the tawney for everyday, or undress. Scarlet embroidered with gold has continued to be associated with Royal liveries, whose costume has made few concessions to the march of fashion since the nineteenth century, a notable exception to this general trend being the battle dress uniforms modelled on contemporary military uniform introduced during the Second World War.

The Wardrobe accounts for the early eighteenth century show that there were, in addition to Footmen, such servants as the Groom of the Great Chamber, the Clerk of the Robes, the Page of the Backstairs and the Page of the

THE MOMENT BEFORE PRESENTATION. Drawing by Arthur Hopkins published in the *Illustrated London News* 2 June 1888. On the left are the Gentlemen at Arms in scarlet coatees and dark blue trousers with gilt helmets. They were as essential to the ceremony as the debutantes.

Presence to be provided with appropriate liveries. Money was also set aside for the issue of liveries to senior officials, such as Sir Christopher Wren, in 1712 Surveyer General of the Works—who at the feast of All Saints was paid £12.75 for his livery. Liveries were given or money paid to recipients on religious anniversaries—Michaelmas, All Saints, St John the Baptist and the feast of St Andrew the Apostle. This was a form of allowance—a 'perk' of the post, and not an actual issue of clothing. There is no doubt that clothing was given to the men of the Yeomen of the Guard. The Yeomen are one of oldest Royal bodyguards in existence, established over five hundred years ago, and still provide a ceremonial guard at the Garden Parties given by the Queen at Buckingham Palace.

In the eighteenth century the Wardrobe was responsible for issuing the Yeomen's clothing. The way in which this happened illustrates the economic impact caused by the supply of court liveries. It provided a regular and almost guaranteed income to certain favoured suppliers in trades ranging from embroiderers to sword cutlers. Regularly 92 Yeomen of the Guard and 40 Yeomen Warders of the Tower of London were equipped. In the 1760s their uniform included a crimson coat and breeches, a black hat, a sword, stockings and shoes. In 1762 the cloth was ordered from Burfoot and Fisher: over 700 yards of crimson cloth for the coats, breeches and belts, and 726 yards of blue serge for linings. Gold lace to embroider the liveries was obtained from Plummer, recorded as a gold laceman: there was narrow gold lace for the coats, breeches and waist belts, and gold breast buttons. Edward Parker was a silk laceman, who supplied broad 'taffety' ribbon for the bands around the bonnets. All of the material then passed to tailors and others for making up. Jacob Alt and Jane Humphries were regular suppliers of Royal Liveries. They made the coats and breeches, edging them with blue velvet and gold arras lace, lining the coats with fustian and the sleeves with blue serge. In common with modern businesses they had their share of labour problems: workers demanding additional payment at a critical point in the production process and the management allowing them an additional £0.15 a suit as a result. Helen Child made the belts and sub-contracted for the supply of the gilt basket hilted swords with silver grips. Sarah Green, embroideress, worked gold bullion roses and thistles—emblematic of the union of Scotland and England—together with the Royal Crown and the letters GR for Georgius Rex on the front and back of the coats. Richard Hotham provided stockings of blue grey, in a large size, Susannah Walsh bonnets of black velvet and Henry Jaffray buckskin gloves. Over £1500 was injected annually into London businesses from the pro-

A VIEW OF THE GARDEN ENTRANCE OF ST JAMES'S PALACE. An engraving showing a Yeoman of the Guard fulfilling his role as Royal Body Guard in preventing Margaret Nicholson from assassinating George III on 2 August 1786.

THE OPENING OF PARLIAMENT—THE SCOTTISH HERALDS PROCEEDING TO THE
CROSS OF EDINBURGH TO MAKE THE ROYAL PROCLAMATION C 1890. Drawing by
B Hall, the Heralds are wearing a distinctive head-dress with their tabards.

vision of liveries for the Yeomen of the Guard and Yeomen Warders, firms such as Alt and Humphries were given orders worth £200.

The same firms supplied liveries for the Children of the Chapel Royal, for The Bargemen and Watermen, the Waterman to the late Queen Caroline's Barge, and three undergamekeepers at the King's House at Newmarket.

The Wardrobe also provided an allowance for the Heralds at the College of Arms. These men, experts in all matters of heraldic arms, family pedigree and ceremony, wore over their court suits (and from 1831 over a uniform, first of blue and then a scarlet coat and blue trousers) a tabard. The tabard is a medieval style of garment, consisting of front and back panels, and hanging sleeves, which are embroidered with the arms of a particular nobleman or in the case of the Royal Heralds, the Royal Arms. Henry Hill, Brunswick Herald in 1762/3 was granted an allowance of £40 for his tabard of

crimson and blue satin, embroidered with gold and silver threads with the King's Arms, and lined with crimson silk.

The issue of livery reached departments and offices of the Royal Household that today seem archaic to say the least. The Rat Killer in Ordinary to King George III had a crimson cloth coat and breeches. Sarah Green embroidered on the coat an appropriate device: the letters GR with the Royal Crown and on the left arm—traditional place for the livery badge—a design of rats with a wheatsheaf. She charged the equivalent of £4.20 in 1763 for the work.

Perhaps the most unusual commission went to those merchants and tradespeople who supplied liveries for the keepers of the elephant presented to the King in 1763. An embroiderer Richard Harrison had made a large blue cloth lined with red baize and fringed with gold to cover the beast. Alt and Humphries made up the suits for the two Indians who had been sent

77

The Magnificent FORM of the PROCESSION usually observed in the CORONATION of the KINGS and QUEENS of ENGLAND.

THE MAGNIFICENT FORM OF THE PROCESSION USUALLY OBSERVED IN THE CORONATION OF THE KINGS AND QUEENS OF ENGLAND. Engraving showing members of the Royal Household in 1690.

Facing page. George V in Windsor Uniform. Painted by Sir Oswald Birley dated 1934. This is the style of Windsor Uniform still worn by certain members of the Royal Family.

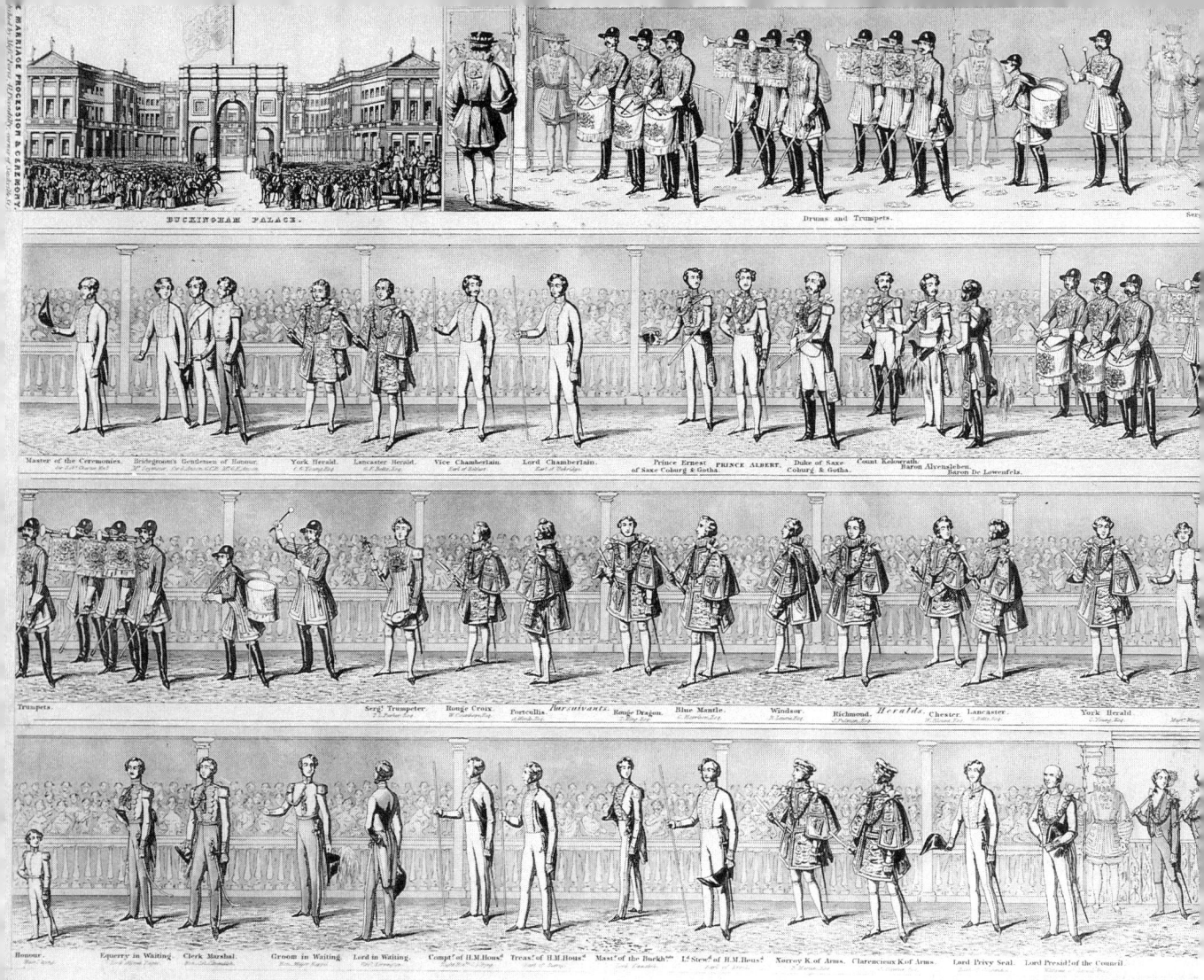

THE MARRIAGE PROCESSION AND CEREMONY
Queen Victoria's marriage to Prince Albert in 1840. One of a series of three engravings showing members of the Royal Household including the Lord Chamberlain in uniform.

with the elephant. The principal elephant keeper had a jacket of blue cloth lined with red serge, waistcoat and trousers of blue lined with flannel, gilt buttons and a rose coloured silk robe and cap, in the Turkish style. His assistant wore a blue jacket lined with yellow with silver buttons, and whereas his superior was given pumps with yellow metal buckles, he had to be content to be shod with shoes with white metal buckles.

All of the clothing so far considered was properly livery: it signified membership of a household, and a position within it. Except in the rather special case of the Heralds' tabards these clothes were confined to the lower parts of the hierarchy of the court, the idea of a distinctive costume travelling only so far up the levels of the administration. It would have been unthinkable for the King's ministers, and his more elevated functionaries to dress in clothing that was in some way emblematic of their work and status. But in the third quarter of the eighteenth century all this was about to change.

In Britain the first court uniform in the sense we should think of the word was the Windsor uniform. There is some reason to believe that

Frederick Prince of Wales had adopted the practice of wearing a form of dress that was peculiar to the Prince and his immediate circle, as a picture of him with a hunting party shows the gentlemen in a costume of dark blue with scarlet cuffs and facings. This was in 1734. By 1780 George III had developed this relatively simple sporting costume into a dark blue coat embroidered with gold, but still with scarlet cuffs and facings, worn with a buff waistcoat and breeches. This was the full dress version of the Windsor uniform, named after the Castle in Berkshire that was the King's favourite residence. Permission to wear the uniform was in the gift of the King, who confined it to his family and the senior court officials.

George III was not the first monarch to borrow from his armies the idea of a uniform costume to be worn at Court. His second cousin Frederick the Great, with whom he shared a love of uniforms, customarily appeared in a costume of similar design, and in 1778 the Swedish king had designed a uniform to be worn at Court by the Royal Family and the officers of the court and government. From the 1780s onwards the British Royal family followed suit. At a court ball to mark the anniversary of the birth of the Prince of Wales the King and the Royal family appeared in the full dress Windsor uniform, and by 1786 Fanny Burney could write that the costume was worn by 'all the men who belong to His Majesty and come into his presence at Windsor'.

There was an undress, or less formal order of the uniform, to be worn on those occasions when the gold embroidery of the full dress would have been inappropriate. This was the 'plain Windsor uniform' worn by the Earl of Ailesbury when in attendance upon the Royal Party on the occasion of a visit paid by an Austrian Archduke in 1786, at Kew Palace, and by the King when visiting Whitbread's brewery in London a year later. This undress version, a plain coat, with the characteristic scarlet collar and cuffs, worn with dark coloured breeches, was to prove more enduring than the more lavish full dress. It was worn by George IV when entertaining a visiting Spanish aristocrat in 1828, and by the young Prince George of Cumberland in 1829. It also appealed to the simple taste of William IV who appeared in it to open the new London Bridge in 1831. During

Queen Victoria's reign the Gentlemen in Waiting and other members of her Houshold wore it at Windsor, at Garden Parties and receptions in the grounds of the Castle. Its use during day time was discontinued shortly before the First World War, but it continues to be worn in evening dress by certain members of the Royal Family.

It was not an exclusively male costume. For example the *Reading Mercury*, reporting a meet of the Royal Staghounds on 25 October 1789, said that the Queen and the Princess Royal wore riding habits of blue with scarlet collar and cuffs. Nor was its use confined always to Britain: Ninian Home, appointed Governor of Grenada in 1793 had his tailors, Douglas and Lambert of St Martin's Lane London make up a coat of the Windsor uniform in thin cloth suitable for tropical wear.

In the Windsor uniform therefore we detect the beginnings of court uniforms in Britain, as distinct from court liveries. To be sure the costume for many contemporaries still signified service—Fanny Burney writes of 'the men who belong to the King', wearing it—but there is another element at work. Like other European Courts the English Court is now attempting to present a unified face, distinct in its relative simplicity from the glittering individualism of the splendid court suits of an earlier period. It is no coincidence that the period that saw the emergence of court uniforms was one of international strife: national armies were being raised and equipped on a vast scale and uniform clothing distinguished one country's forces from anothers, and as the armed forces became an important focus of national life, so the idea of uniform clothing spread from the military to the civilian at Court.

Again, as with the Windsor uniform, developments of other court uniforms in Britain were not taking place in isolation. Countries with a stronger military tradition put their Courts in uniform first: in Sweden, Russia and Austria in the last quarter of the eighteenth century special uniforms for government and Royal Household officials were being designed and it is within this context that the emergence of the Civil Uniform in Britain must be placed.

The Prince of Wales, George III's eldest son, later Prince Regent, shared with his father, a

Joseph Alexander von Hübner 1878 in Austrian court uniform; painted by C von Blaas. Although similar in many respects, the costume differs from the contemporary British style in that the coatee is worn open with white tie and waistcoat.

passionate interest in military uniforms. During the first decade of the nineteenth century he would have been aware of developments in court uniforms by his brother monarchs and by the man who threatened them all—Napoleon 1. The Prince had already in 1783 had a uniform designed for his attendants of blue and buff, (symbolic of the Whig political interest), so it was natural he should turn his attention to the question of clothing his advisors, sometime after he became Regent in 1811. He probably had a number of designs submitted for his approval, perhaps even a number of patterns made up. He decided upon a uniform that was heavily influenced by the costume of marshals in the French Army: the British Civil Uniform being a dark blue wool coatee, a garment cut across horizontally at the waist, with tails behind, which buttoned up the front and was single breasted, worn with white or buff breeches, stockings and court pumps. A hat with an ostrich feather border and a sword with a gilt hilt, its design based on the contemporary court sword, completed the outfit. The most notable feature about the costume was however the lavish use of gold wire embroidery in a pattern of stylized oakleaves, acorns and palmettes. These elements were part of the fashionable vocabulary of embroidery for court uniforms elsewhere in Europe. A design incorporating symbols of durability and

Royal Household. Full dress uniform, 3rd Class c 1910. This is distinguished from the Civil Uniform by the scarlet collar and cuffs. The class is denoted by the width and form of the gold embroidery.

MARSHALLING THE PROCESSION OF THE BRIDE
An engraving of the ceremonies associated with the marriage of the Prince of
Wales to Princess Alexandra of Denmark 1863, showing the Princess in St
George's Chapel, Windsor, with (on the left) Heralds and the Royal Body
Guard.

resolution was appropriate for a costume of this
nature.

The significance of the pattern of the garment
was perhaps lost on some of those whose position obliged them to wear the uniform: marked
reluctance was noted by the Prince Regent
amongst some of his ministers, and he went out
of his way at a reception to praise Mr Planta (a
relatively junior official in the Foreign Office),
who he saw wearing the uniform, which, as he
declared loudly, his ministers generally refused
to wear.

There were probably two reasons for this
unenthusiastic attitude. One was undoubtedly
cost. Creevey, the noted diarist, expressed to
Lord Grey his reluctance to appear at Court in
1831, because he thought he would have to pay
£120 for the appropriate uniform. Grey assured
him that this was the cost of the most elabora-
tely embroidered Privy Councillors uniform—
that prescribed for Creevey would cost only
£40. A more fundamental objection may have
been that uniform was still regarded solely as a
form of livery. Significantly Creevey refers to
his uniform as 'my new livery', and liveries were
identified as the dress of domestic servants.

84

There was in addition the difficulty of knowing what exactly constituted the correct uniform on various occasions. To be presented to the King, at a Levee, pantaloons and boots were worn, with the coatee, but at a Drawing Room at which the Queen was present, Creevey had to wear white breeches, knee buckles, silk stockings and shoes with gilt buckles. The fact that in May 1831 the Lord Chamberlain's Office had to issue two sets of instructions clarifying when pantaloons and boots and when breeches with stockings and shoes were to be worn, indicates a degree of confusion about the matter. Since all sovereigns seem to have had a sharp eye for the incorrect manner of dress, a certain amount of trepidation would be understandable. George IV once spied Lord John Russell in uniform, but without the aiguillette hanging from his shoulder, which was required for his position. He called out that he supposed Russell was a regimental doctor, in the context of the time indicating disgust at the sartorial omission.

The suite of the Italian Ambassador, photographed at the New Year's Reception, Paris 1912. The Ambassador, His Excellency Cavaliere Tommaso Tittoni, is shown centre front.

A Herald c 1820. Coloured engraving.
The Herald wears a tabard
embroidered with the Royal Coat of
Arms, incorporating the White Horse
of Hanover.

Despite the initially lukewarm reaction to the
new Civil Uniform the development of the
clothing continued: gold lace stripes on the full
dress breeches were abandoned during the reign
of William IV, and gradually more and more
officials found the idea of wearing a specific
costume to court to their liking. Indeed by 1846
so great was the demand on the part of relatively
minor functionaries that Queen Victoria had a
fifth class of the uniform designed.

With Civil Uniform each position within a
government department, down to a relatively
junior level, was assigned a class—so that the
Secretary of State would be entitled to the
highest, first or Privy Councillor's order of
dress, and a less exalted official, such as the
Précis Writer in the Office of the Foreign Secretary would have worn the fifth class. The uniform was described in great detail in the various
editions of a publication that was entitled *Dress
Worn at Court*, and an early edition of 1882
brought together many separately printed regulations concerning gentlemen's court dress and
uniforms. In this the first class embroidery was
five inches wide, the fifth three-eights. The last
edition of *Dress Worn at Court* was published in
1937. To determine which class one was
allowed, the *Schedules of Civil Uniform* had to be
consulted. These listed the ministries and departments and within them the classification of
officials who worked there.

The 1903 *Dress Worn at Court* lists in addition
to the Civil Service over forty different departments, offices and appointments which had particular costumes prescribed to them. There were
two related influences on the design of the
costumes. Most potent was that of military
uniform and allied to this the conservatism that
is characteristic of much ceremonial and formal
costume. The uniforms worn by Lords Lieutenant and their Deputies are a good example of
the persistent military influence. The Lieutenants were the monarch's representatives in
the counties and historically had had responsibilities for local defence. In the 1830s they were
allowed a new uniform which appears to have
been modelled on that currently worn by
general officers in the Army—the sword for
Lieutenants of County was of the same pattern.
The Gentlemen's Magazine of Fashion commented
upon the new Deputy Lieutenants' uniform in
1832 'a regimental coat and gold trappings

[have] been attached to the appointment'. This was felt to be 'an easy way of playing soldiers' and 'at the Levee we may expect a crowd of these fine feathered birds (a reference to the plumes in the head-dress) jostling against general officers'.

Governor Generals, representing the sovereign in the colonies, originally wore the Civil Uniform. In 1903 they were allowed a coat based on the frock coat worn in undress by general officers, with the hat and trousers modelled on those for Lords Lieutenant. By 1912 they had their own full dress uniform prescribed, which was very similar to that for Lieutenants but in dark blue cloth and with a silver aiguillette attached to the shoulder.

The uniform had by the beginning of the twentieth century left the demands of practical soldiering far behind—the coatee, for example, was abolished for most of the army in 1855. It was designed to impress, to confer status and power on the wearer—it had nothing to do with his personality. Court dress, like military clothing, was designed to diminish or ignore the individual in favour of the office.

Military inspired uniforms were prescribed during the reign of William IV for Royal Bodyguards. The officers of both the Honourable Corps of Gentlemen at Arms and the Yeomen of the Guard had new uniforms ordered for them by the King. Both were to wear the scarlet coatee with stand collar, blue black trousers and epaulettes currently in vogue in the regular army. The Royal Company of Archers had had the status of royal bodyguard conferred upon them at the time of the visit paid to Scotland by George IV in 1822. For some time during his reign their uniform for Court consisted of a scarlet coat with green collar and cuffs, embroidered with thistles and arrows, a white waistcoat and breeches with court shoes. In 1831 this elegant attire was altered. A green cloth coatee with green velvet collar and cuffs embroidered in gold and green trousers with a gold lace stripe was substituted. This court uniform did not change radically until 1937, when alterations were made to the buttoning of the coatee, the head-dress and shoulder ornaments. Royal bodyguard's court uniforms are like so many other court uniforms since the 1830s, particularly good examples of the fossilization of a fashion, unchanging with the times, their very

The King's Body Guard for Scotland (Royal Company of Archers) court dress uniform c 1912. The thistle embroidery indicates the status of the company as Royal Body Guard in Scotland.

Deputy Lieutenant of an Irish County
c 1890. A photograph showing the
shamrock, embroidered in silver wire
on collar and cuffs which was
emblematic of the office.

conservatism expressing faith in tradition and history rather than the contemporary world. The person obliged to wear these costumes had of course more pressing concerns than to reflect upon the psychological implications of a style; all he needed to know was how to obtain them and what it would cost him.

Once invited to a Levee the aspiring civil servant, or newly appointed Lord Lieutenant would visit a tailor conversant with the requirements of court dress—one who had the latest edition of *Dress Worn at Court*. He would be measured for his uniform, his official status checked against the *Schedules of Civil Uniform*, and a sub-contract let to a gold laceman to supply the tailor with the correct amount of gold wire embroidery. This would be added to the coat when it was fitted. Ede and Ravenscroft were at one time in the forefront of the business of supplying court uniforms, and are to this day official robemakers for the legal profession and

for the Orders of Knighthood. From them it was possible to obtain all that was required to outfit the gentlemen for Court. In 1912 the Rt Hon Charles O'Connor bought from Ede and Ravenscroft a Privy Councillor's full and levee dress uniform. This consisted of the coat, lined with silk, richly embroidered with gold and with gilt buttons up the front and on the back skirts, a pair of fine white wool breeches, a pair of white silk stockings and a pair of white cotton stockings (both worn, cotton beneath silk to prevent the flesh colour of the legs showing), a set of gilt shoe and knee buckles, a sword belt, a levee dress coat and trousers, a cocked hat, a cloak and an 'extra size' case to contain the outfit. The cost was nearly £170. A significant proportion of this cost would have been for the gold embroidery. For example, when altering a uniform to the second class, and therefore having to add embroidery to an existing uniform, the cost was £37.

88

Ambassador's full dress uniform c 1900. A view showing the gold embroidery on the seams of the sleeves and the back of the coat. Ths is a more elaborate version of the Civil uniform.

Embroidery for Civil Uniforms 1921. An illustration from *Dress Worn at Court* showing how the use of gold embroidery distinguishes the classes of uniform.

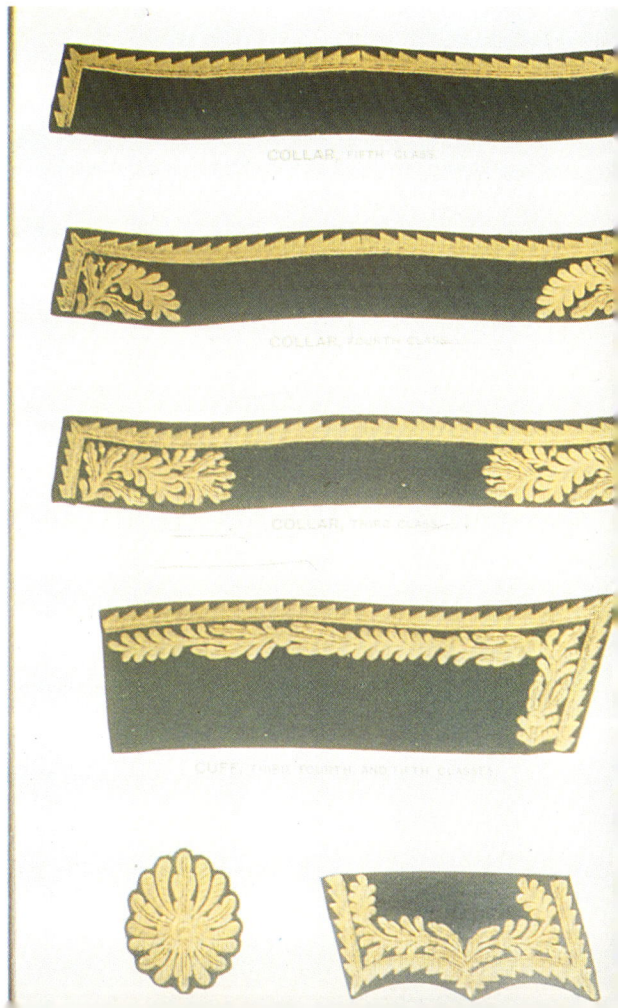

Governors General of Colonies. Full
dress uniform 1912. An illustration
from *Dress Worn at Court*.

Civil Uniform. Full and Levee dress
1912. An illustration from *Dress Worn
at Court*. Full dress was worn at
Evening Courts.

Chinese diplomatic Uniform c 1914.
Design for the embroidery of the cuffs
as provided for the 'laceman'
responsible for the work. The
Uniforms were made by Ede and
Ravenscroft Limited.

Facing page. ROYAL BODY GUARD H M
CORPS OF GENTLEMEN AT ARMS 1861.
Engraving showing various orders of
dress and undress uniform. Full dress
was worn with plumed gilt metal
helmets and scarlet coatees.

There were those for whom this expense was a hard cross to bear. When the first Labour administration came to power it was composed of men for whom this would be true: King George V was however gratified to learn that his ministers would wear court uniforms, and the politicians were informed of a reliable firm that would hire them out—Moss Bros.

It is worthwhile stepping back from the world of the British Court uniform for a moment, to appreciate that developments in Britain had been paralleled throughout the world. The only exception amongst the great powers before the First World War in the rush to gold embroidery and court uniforms had been the United States. Diplomatic uniforms of many nations glittered at the levees at St James's Palace, and English tailors were able to supply foreign as well as British uniforms. In 1912 the Chinese Republic issued regulations for the uniforms that were to be worn by its diplomats and consuls. The coat, cut in the same manner as the British Civil Uniform and of similar fine blue wool cloth, was embroidered with corn sheaves in gold. It had nine large gilt buttons up the front engraved with the letters RC (Republique Chinoise) in the centre, surrounded by the Chinese motif symbolizing five blessings. Lew Yuk Lin, Chinese minister in 1913, wore this skilful blend of occidental and oriental design and paid £102 for it (including 10% discount for cash).

The essentially masculine flavour of court uniforms must have been best savoured at the Levee, at which gentlemen were received by the monarch, or another member of the Royal Family. Courtiers in old age recollected the difficulty of kissing Queen Victoria's hand. The skill in kissing the Royal hand lay in not raising it to one's own lips, but lowering the head to the proferred hand. When the Prince of Wales took responsibility for the Levees he shook hands, initially with all present, an exhausting procedure since over 1000 gentlemen might attend, later only ambassadors were so favoured.

Percy Armytage, writing in 1927, felt that the levee was probably the most interesting of all court ceremonies. They were 'an epitome of history and of the Empire', attended by the Diplomatic Corps in all their various uniforms, statesmen, civil servants in the various classes of uniform, 'men who have grown old in public

THE FIRST LEVEE OF EDWARD VII AT THE PALACE OF HOLYROODHOUSE
Painting by Dickinson c 1902. The Royal Body Guard is provided by the
Royal Company of Archers.

George Byng, Page of Honour c 1880, photographed by Lombardi and
Company wearing a scarlet coat edged with gold lace, a waistcoat of white
satin and white breeches.

Civil uniform, full dress 1912. Detail of embroidery on the cuff. The cost of this work was a significant element in the total price of the uniform.

THE ROYAL COMPANY OF ARCHERS LEAVING THE PALACE OF HOLYROODHOUSE WITH PIPERS AND DRUMMERS OF THE ROYAL SCOTS 19 August 1886. Painted in water colour by W Cumming. The mounted figure is the Marquess of Lothian, Captain General of the Royal Company.

HIS MAJESTY'S LIEUTENANTS OF COUNTIES.

FULL DRESS.

life and public service elbow beardless boys wearing their first uniforms'.

The last Levee at St James's took place in 1939. Court uniforms are still worn at such occasions as the State Opening of Parliament but the demand for such uniforms is only a shadow of what it was even fifty years ago. As these costumes outlive both their usefulness and in some cases their owners, they occasionally find their way to auction, and other outlets where the curious may buy them as a form of fancy dress. Twenty years ago there was an interest in gold braid and lace in the context of fancy dress, and there are recorded instances of people who would have been unlikely to require uniforms for Court, appearing in circumstances that were certainly not courtly in the fine wool and gold embroidery of the civil and other uniforms. The self proclaimed iconoclasts of the 1960s found an affinity in their flirtation with uniforms designed a century and a half before, with the Prince Regent who in some ways might have found it all very reprehensible, but in others perhaps understandable.

Lord Lieutenants of County. Full dress uniform 1912. An illustration from *Dress Worn at Court*.

CHAPTER FIVE

'Farewell Dear Debs'

The Twentieth Century

The Queen magazine noted in 1905 'Between the Drawing Rooms of the Victorian reign and the Courts of Edward VII and Queen Alexandra there is very little in common'. The refrain so frequently heard in 1900 and 1901 'there was a great deal of black worn' and 'the Throne Room presented a very funeral aspect' gives way to descriptions of 'an exceptionally brilliant spectacle'.

The new reign saw significant changes in the ceremonial employed at Buckingham Palace. The timing of the Courts was radically altered, as the afternoon Drawing Rooms were abandoned in favour of Evening Courts, much to the delight of the participants. Whether or not this was the result of the 'Plaintive appeal' on behalf of the debutantes published in the *Illustrated London News*, in 1901, is not recorded:

> When we attend a Drawing Room
> We want to wear our evening bloom
> For evening sheds a gentle ray
> That makes amends for cruel day
> O Gracious Queen, give kindly light
> And let us flock to you by night

For those attending Courts the Palace was open to guests at 9 o'clock in the evening, the formal reception commencing at 10 o'clock. About half an hour later 'there was a rustle which betokened an entry of importance and the members of the suites and Royal Household passed to their places ... then to the strains of the National Anthem came the King and Queen'.

Edward VII favoured what were known as 'Open Courts' on the pattern then used in Prussia and the German states. As *The Queen* magazine explained 'those who were bidden with their invitation received an intimation that

only those who were presented and the ladies presenting young girls were to pass the Royal presence in the usual manner ... were gathered together in a separate apartment'. They were joined by those who had the 'entrée' and ambassadors and other favoured guests. The remainder of the company congregated in the State Apartments. After the formal Presentation had taken place the members of the Royal Family progressed through their guests exchanging greetings. These receptions could last into the early hours of the morning. On one occasion the Royal Party did not arrive until half past eleven.

It was noted that compared with the complicated etiquette required at an Afternoon Presentation under Queen Victoria, the ceremonial content of an Evening Court was 'child's play'. Despite the fact that the vast and imposing ballroom had been made into the new Throne Room, the access and orientation of the room meant that those being presented could enter, pass directly in a straight line in front of the dias occupied by the Royal party and then withdraw through a doorway immediately opposite. This was easier than having to be directed by one of the court officials present. Moreover where in the previous reign there might be more than a dozen members of the Royal Family standing *'en grande tenue'* to all of whom obeisance had to be made, under Edward VII and his successors only two curtseys had to be made: one to the King and one to the Queen. The debutante welcomed this relaxation, as any modification in the complex ritual of Presentation helped the nervous.

The new decorations at Buckingham Palace, illuminated with additional electric lighting must have appeared very splendid to the guests. There were elaborate hangings of red velvet

Three debutante sisters dressed for Court. Photograph c 1906. Court trains at
this date could be extremely long and were lavishly decorated.

Court dress worn by Lady Pearson 1908. The dress is of silk, trimmed with lace and silver gauze ribbon, made by Jay's of Regent Street.

Court dress worn by Lady Lyle 1908. The dress is of satin embroidered with silks with a velvet train, made by Jay's of Regent Street.

The Hon Charlotte Knollys, Woman of the Bedchamber to Queen Alexandra
in court dress c 1902. Photograph by Ward D Downey.

A PRESENTATION AT COURT: A DEBUTANTE CURTSEYING TO THEIR MAJESTIES THE
KING AND QUEEN. Painted by W Hatherell c 1905.

embroidered with the Royal Arms and enormous flower arrangements of lilies, geraniums,
palms and ferns which had previously only been
brought out for Court Balls. The effect was
designed to 'throw into greater prominence the
scarlet uniforms of officials . . . in marked contrast to the white plumes and veils of the ladies'.

Full court dress was of course imperative for
all ladies attending an Evening Court. In the
words of The Queen in 1903 this consisted of
'low bodice, short sleeves and train to [the]
dress, from three and a half to four and a half
yards in length . . . it is also imperative to wear
court plumes which consist for a married lady of
three white feathers and two white ostrich
feathers for an unmarried lady, white veils of

tulle or lace lappets to be worn with the
feathers'.

It was also suggested that white was the most
appropriate colour for dresses for both debutantes and married ladies, enlivened with coloured flowers and foliage. For the second Court
of 1903 Queen Alexandra chose to wear 'white
satin covered with soft silver spangled chiffon'
which set off very well the sash of the Order of
the Garter and the Queen's splendid diamonds.

With the accession of Edward VII it had been
proposed initially that only those being presented and those presenting them should wear
trains with their dresses. This order was re-
scinded before the first of the 'Open Courts' was
held and the only ladies not wearing trains were

Court dress worn by Lady Amelia Fraser c 1910. Lady Amelia wears half mourning. In the background may be seen the uniforms worn by an Ambassador and the Superintendent of the Royal Mews c 1910.

Lady Warmington in court dress c 1922. Photograph by Bassano. She wears the modified style of court train, much shorter in length than pre-War examples.

those who had not had time to prepare them. The carrying of bouquets remained optional.

As in the previous century ladies in deep mourning were permitted to wear black dresses and feathers and could choose either grey or black gloves. If elderly, infirm, or ill, they might, on application to the Lord Chamberlain's Office, be allowed to wear 'High Court Dress' with sleeves and a higher neckline than normally permitted. All of these regulations were drawn together in the 1908 edition of *Dress worn at Court*, ladies now being taken within the orbit of this publication which had previously confined itself to gentlemen's court dress.

In addition to presentations at Buckingham Palace there were those at the Palace of Holyroodhouse, in Edinburgh. The retiming of the English Courts did not affect them, and Afternoon Presentation Parties were retained, at which afternoon dress and hats were worn. In 1903 the Hon Mrs Thomas Watson chose to

wear a dress of white silk flounced with chiffon and draped with Brussels lace. Her hat was a white tulle toque decorated with sprays of white heather, and she carried a large bouquet of roses. Acceptance of this informality was not universal. It was said one lady contrived at a presentation at Holyroodhouse, to place a large diamond tiara on top of her toque!

Edward VII was succeeded in 1910 by his son George V. The Courts of the new reign were greeted enthusiastically by *The Queen*: 'The Courts, the Courts, the whole air rings with the cry . . . the world is aflutter with preparations over the most sumptuous gowns.' There was a slight adjustment to the timing too, which would have been welcome: the Royal Party now entered at 9.30 pm which allowed the company to retire to the supper room after the conclusion of the ceremonies by midnight.

Queen Mary was clearly concerned that standards of dress should be maintained at Court:

MISS EDWARDS.   [Speaight Ltd.

GOWN WORN BY MISS CHADWYCK-HEALEY.

MISS WINIFRED WOODBINE PARISH.   [Speaight Ltd.

GOWN WORN BY MRS ECKSTEIN.

Photographs and drawings of dresses
worn to Court, published in *The Queen*
February 1913.

Photograph of Miss Maud Hyde
arriving at Buckingham Palace for
presentation in June 1926. She was
presented by Lady Blades.

she let it be known before her first Court that
the tight skirts recently popular with the Paris
couture houses would not be considered appropriate for the British Court. This caused problems for those ladies who had already bought
their gowns but even with the restriction the
Courts were particularly splendid. The dress
worn by Lady Diana Manners, youngest
daughter of the Duke and Duchess of Rutland
at the second Court of the new reign aroused
great interest. It was of ivory net over ivory
brocaded crêpe de chine ornamented with a
silver waistband. Lady Diana described the
dress as 'adequate', but the train, which she had
designed herself, she considered much more
impressive. This consisted of three yards of
cream net sprinkled generously with pink rose
petals, each attached by a diamond dewdrop.
Lady Sackville at the third Court of the year
wore blue satin veiled with emerald green chiffon, the chiffon embroidered with satin leaves,
with a train of emerald green tissue veiled and
festooned with chiffon and leaves. She presented
her daughter the Hon Victoria Sackville-West
who wore a gown of white satin, the bodice
arranged with Buckingham lace and chiffon, the
train satin, festooned with silver bows and tulle.

This catalogue of extravagance was to come
to an abrupt end in 1914 when grimmer events
demanded the attention of King and country.
On 15 August *The Queen* reported 'A fortnight
ago the social world of England was on its way
to Cowes, yachts were being fitted out and
everyone was looking forward to the autumn

Court dress worn by Miss Dorothy Holman 1914 and a court uniform worn by the King's Body Guard for Scotland (Royal Company of Archers) c 1914.

Mr and Mrs Ronald Cross in court dress c 1927. Photograph by Bassano. Mrs Cross carries a large fashionable ostrich feather fan while her husband wears velvet court dress (new style).

with the holiday feeling that prevails everywhere at the end of a London Season. The unlooked for events of last week have changed everything . . .'. Britain declared war on Germany on 4 August 1914, and amongst the unlooked for consequences of the First World War was the disappearance of several European Courts, the monarchies that were their focus being swept away in the War and its immediate aftermath.

The British monarchy was more durable but as no Courts were held during the War, there was a substantial backlog of those awaiting presentation to the monarch, on its conclusion. War as an agent of social change does not seem at first sight to have materially affected the *raison d'être* of the Court, although it had perhaps begun to set in motion long-term changes in British society which were to take a generation to emerge.

In 1919 the Lord Chamberlain's Office was faced with the problem of arranging the presentation of far more young ladies than could be accommodated at Evening Courts. It was decided that Afternoon Garden Parties should be held during July 1919. There would be no individual presentations and all those who would have made their curtseys were informed that they should consider themselves correctly presented by virtue of their attendance at one of these gatherings. Afternoon dress was prescribed, and *The Queen* faithfully recorded the scene 'short dresses were the order of the day, but not too short. One young girl clad in satin had flounces of ostrich feathers one above the other from the hem to the waist . . . there was an immense variety of headgear, the feathers often congregated round the outside brim of the hat, Birds of Paradise proudly uprearing above the crowns of many others . . . lace skirts peeped

The Misses M and V Lyttleton in court
dress c 1927. Photograph by Bassano.
The feather and veil head-dress and
court trains conform to regulation but
neither sister is wearing gloves.

through panels of silk or chiffon and many
debutantes wore the most diaphanous gowns of
georgette . . .'.

The Afternoon Parties were clearly not as
sumptuous as the Evening Courts, the return of
which was eagerly anticipated the following
year. After an interval of over five years there
was consternation among ladies as to the correct
dress. Gentlemen of course could appear in their
uniforms or suits according to regulation. The
Lord Chamberlain's Office once more resolved
the problem, after receiving a considerable correspondence on the matter. It prepared illustrations of 'approved' gowns, suitable for 'the
three ages of woman'. The designs showed
significant departures from tradition. It was
now suggested that the debutante might appear
in pale blue rather than the conventional pre-
war white, with a floral wreath ornamenting the
hair. Older women were prescribed a gown
with a 'wispy tail', in place of the court train.

The effect of these changes in ladies dress was
to alter the appearance of the Courts, giving
them the air of a stately evening party. They also
served to throw the Queen into a new prominence since she alone wore the long train to her
dress. In 1920 Queen Mary wore a dress that
had 'the finest bead embroidery, flashing now
rose, now tender green, now sunset gold, now
the white of hoar frost, with long fronds of Nile
green and silver brocade falling from the
shoulders'.

Further external events affected the Court a
year later. The coal strike prevented the holding
of the Evening Courts, so that as in 1919,
Garden Parties were held and as on the earlier
occasion Afternoon Dress was worn. Obviously
concerned at the time it was taking for the
Evening Courts to become once more firmly
established as the brilliant centrepiece of the
Season, the fashionable journals of 1922 made
oblique pleas for their restoration, citing the
benefit to the dressmaking trades. There was the
difference too for the debutante of making her
curtsey in a gown especially prescribed for the
occasion. Doubtless to the delight of trade and
Society alike, in May the Lord Chamberlain's
Office issued a full schedule of ladies court
dress. The 'wispy tail' of 1920 disappeared in
favour of a modified court train, now firmly
restricted in length to eighteen inches from the
heel of the wearer. Ostrich feathers and a tulle

Lady Anne Walpole in court dress
1939. Photograph by Bassano. Lady
Anne wears a crinoline style dress of
white lace. She was voted one of the
prettiest debutantes of the 1939
Season.

veil or lappets were reintroduced for the head-
dress, the feathers to be arranged in a manner
suggestive of the three feathers of the crest of
the Prince of Wales.

The fashion for short bobbed hair in the
1920s caused mothers of debutantes concern
with regard to the securing of the feathers.
There were several solutions. Monsieur Jean
Stehr, a hairdresser, advocated the adoption of
styles which left the crown of the head free from
curls or waves. Alternatively the feathers could
be tucked into the back of the tiara, which was
now worn low over the forehead.

Fashion changed faster than the editions of
the Lord Chamberlain's Regulations and by
1928 *The Queen* was noting several startling
deviations from the prescribed dress. Prominent
amongst these eccentricities was the grass green
gown and matching veil worn by one lady, and
even more startling to behold, the 'magpie'
dress. The inspiration for this outfit seems to
have been the permitted dress for mourning,
when a woman could wear black with black veil
and feathers—but in this case, deciding on a
compromise of black and white the lady
appeared at Court in black and white feathers,
with a veil that was one half black, one half
white, and a dress too that was black and white.
Other ladies wore up to six feathers in place of
the regulation three, and one who, perhaps
feeling that the combination of higher hemline
with train was a little absurd, emphasized the
incongruity by wearing a very short dress with a
train of excessive length. The reissuing of Regulations in 1929, which restated the requirements
for ladies costume at Court, may have been a
response to the liberal interpretation of earlier
rules, and curbed such excesses.

Significant changes in court dress and ceremonial occurred during the brief reign of
Edward VIII. He chose to hold two Afternoon
Presentation parties in 'July 1936. Attendance
was restricted to debutantes and those ladies
who wished to make presentations, as opposed
to the larger gatherings of 1919 and 1921. The
King sat under a red and gold canopy supported
on silver posts, and the debutantes curtseyed
before him. It was the Lord Chamberlain, rather
than the sponsor, who presented the lady.

The Parties were looked forward to with
great anticipation. The beautiful gardens at
Buckingham Palace, it was felt, would provide

Afternoon dress worn by Mrs James Fraser to one of the two Presentation Garden Parties held by Edward VIII in 1936. The dress was purchased from Jay's Limited of Regent Street. Mrs Fraser presented her daughters Jean and Iona.

A TYPICAL COURT DRESS 1926. Illustration from *Dress Worn at Court* 1929. The design was by Messrs Reville & Co and shows the higher hemline of the period.

an excellent foil to the pretty afternoon dresses of the debutantes. Unfortunately a serious miscalculation had been made with respect to the vagaries of the English weather. During the first afternoon it rained very heavily: the refreshment marquees could not shelter everyone and became crowded almost to the point of suffocation. Dresses and hats suffered. Those attending the second afternoon party were careful to wear raincoats and carry umbrellas. As *The Queen* remarked 'it is quite certain that the last has now been heard of these Royal Afternoon Receptions'.

Evening Courts resumed with the accession of George VI and Queen Elizabeth. Long dresses, the train as established in 1922, ostrich feathers and veil were all prescribed in the 1937 edition of *Dress to be worn at Court*. The debutante, accompanied by her sponsor would arrive at Buckingham Palace for 8.30pm. Clutching the pink card that was their 'passport' to the Throne Room they made their way up the staircase to a waiting room. An usher would

then appear to announce 'Ladies will you come now, Ladies have you all your cards?' There was a walk along a passage to the door of the Throne Room where trains were dropped. The sponsor entered first, curtseyed to the King and then the Queen while the usher called out the name of the appropriate debutante who followed. She then curtseyed and accompanied by her sponsor passed from the Throne Room to the Blue Drawing Room.

The Queen wrote in March 1939 'It would be a sad day for Great Britain if this yearly ceremony of young people making their obeisance to their Majesties and in return receiving the official recognition of the head of the Royal Family was ever done away with.' Lady Anne Walpole, wearing a crinoline dress of white lace, was voted one of the prettiest of the 1939 debutantes. Would she, together with her contemporaries Miss Margaret Maxwell-Lyte, Miss Cynthia Joseph and Miss Rosemary Beale-Brown have realized that the outbreak of the Second World War in September of that year

Sir John and Lady Birchell dressed for an Evening Court c 1928. Photograph by Bassano. Sir John wears full dress Hussar uniform. Lady Birchell's tiara is placed low over the forehead following the fashionable mode.

was to bring about an abrupt end to the Season for 1939, and for several years to come, as well as consigning to history the Evening Courts and levees?

Gentlemen's dress, worn to Courts and Levees, was not as subject to the changes of fashion as that of ladies. The six editions of *Dress worn at Court*, which appeared between 1903 and 1937 recorded for the most part only minor changes to the uniforms that had been developed during the nineteenth century. For those men who were not entitled to uniform, velvet court dress was usually worn. There is in addition a description of an informal court dress, suitable for wear at dinners, balls and receptions as an alternative to civil uniform. The coat was similar to that worn for ordinary evening wear with silk revers, and was worn with a black or white waistcoat and black cloth or stockinette breeches. An evening shirt with white tie, plain court shoes and a folded cocked hat or opera hat completed the costume.

The uniforms for those entitled to wear them altered very little. The full dress uniform for Lords Lieutenant changed from a coatee in 1903 to a tunic in 1920. This abandonment of the tailed garment was some way behind the uniform of general officers. An undress version in service dress khaki, modelled closely on the service dress of officers of the period, was introduced towards the end of the First World War, ornaments known as gorget patches, of blue cloth with a line of crimson gimp, distinguishing the wearer as a Lord Lieutenant. Again following contemporary military practice in the 1950s the scarlet full dress was finally abandoned and a uniform based on the Army's blue cloth No.1 dress substituted.

The relative stagnation of the development of court uniforms should not be thought to imply lack of interest on the part of the monarch: rather the reverse. Both Edward VII and in particular George V had detailed knowledge of the minutiae of uniforms and correct appearance, and ensured standards were maintained. George V is said upon one occasion to have remarked to the Aga Khan that it offended him to see an order out of place on a uniform as much as it would a man in the street to see someone with his shirt outside his trousers. At Court two officials were stationed at the foot of the staircase to see that everyone was correctly

Instruction in the court curtsey, May 1925. This debutante is practising the correct posture at Fiffirella's in London.

dressed before entering the Royal presence. When the American Ambassador insisted upon wearing trousers and not knee breeches to court efforts were made to have the Prince of Wales persuade him otherwise—but to no avail. Fortunately the King was ill upon the occasion of the appearance of the trousered iconoclast. Queen Mary is said to have remarked on seeing the Ambassador 'Papa will not be pleased'.

At the Presentation Garden Parties different orders of dress were worn. The men in 1919 wore top hats, frock coats, white waistcoats, the King setting the example, with a white flower in his buttonhole. Apart from the King's Marshal-men, who stood at the entrance in their military style uniform, there was, according to *The Queen*, 'an entire absence of the crimson and gold liveries and uniforms . . .'.

Ceremonial was slightly different too under George VI. Matters seem to have been speeded up. Gentlemen arriving for a levee at St James's at 11.30 were instructed by a State Page to 'pass out quickly'. The last passed out in 1939, and although presentations of debutantes were revived in 1947, there were to be no more Levees.

The importance of the Court was not confined however to those immediately concerned

Velvet Court Dress (New Style) and a court dress c 1935. The dress is of ivory lace ornamented with gold thread and trimmed with blue ribbon. The train is blue panne velvet and gold lamé.

LIBERTY & CO
REGENT STREET, LONDON, AND PARIS

COLOURED SKETCHES OF MODELS WITH ESTIMATES POST FREE

SPECIALITIES IN THE WORLD-RENOWNED LIBERTY FABRICS

DESIGNERS AND MAKERS OF EVENING DRESSES AND
COURT GOWNS

Advertisement for Liberty & Co. 1912. In common with several other leading stores Liberty was well known for their court dresses.

with the presentations: the social and economic impact of the season spread far beyond the sumptuous confines of Buckingham Palace.

The most obvious impact was the effect felt by the couture houses and department stores which in the months of the year leading up to the season did a lively trade in presentation dresses. As 'Filomena' remarked on the 'Ladies Page' of the *Illustrated London News* in 1901, 'Thousands of people depend for the chief income of their year on the briskness of business in the London Season, which court ceremonies so greatly assist.' Most debutantes and their mothers could not afford to wait until the summons to a Court arrived before selecting an appropriate dress. This was prudent: while a few girls might be disappointed not to receive the expected summons, others, if they had waited until the invitation arrived three weeks before the Court would have found the dressmaking establishments unable to complete the work required in time.

The Parisian 'houses' as well as the English

could be called upon to undertake commissions. The French businesses would be prepared to cut the excesses of fashion in line with Royal dictate. Fashionable magazines describe dresses by Worth, Doucet, Caillot Soeurs and Pacquin amongst others. Mrs Curre's gown by Pacquin in 1914 was of black taffeta worked with grey and silver crystals, the sleeves and upper part of the bodice of tulle embroidered with crystals. Poiret in 1927 designed the dress for the Hon Mrs Mason for her presentation upon marriage. It was of gold lamé and gold lace embroidered with seed pearls and silver beads. The train was also of gold lamé.

English designers after 1900 tended to gravitate less to Paris as the fashionable centre and instead established their own businesses in London. The first house of international repute to be based in London was that of Lucille; it was joined in 1906 by Reville and Rossiter, set up by two buyers from the department store Jay's. By 1910 they had been appointed couturiers to Queen Mary, receiving the prestigious commis-

The Hon Sallyann Vivian with her mother 1949. Sallyann was deb of the year and is photographed on her way to Buckingham Palace to be presented at an Afternoon Presentation Party.

sion of designing the Queen's coronation dress. Royal patronage continued; in 1922 they designed the wedding dress worn by Princess Mary, the Princess Royal, for her marriage with Viscount Lascelles and provided Edwina Ashley with her trousseau for her marriage with Lord Mountbatten. Norman Hartnell had by 1923 made the decision to set up his own house. After two years, with the assistance of a former member of the staff of Molyneux and a French 'first hand', he was attracting the attention of the fashionable world. This resulted in commissions for the court dresses of Barbara Cartland in 1927 and Nancy Beaton in 1928. Nancy Beaton's dress was of layered white silk tulle embroidered with diamond shaped groups of silver sequins. It was not until 1935 however that Hartnell designed a dress for a member of the Royal Family. His first Royal client was Lady Alice Montagu-Douglas-Scott, daughter of the 7th Duke of Buccleuch, shortly to marry the Duke of Gloucester. Hartnell also made the dress which she wore to the 1937 coronation. This was of cream satin, embroidered with an ostrich feather pattern in gold and silver sequins and seed pearls with a gold lamé train.

Other designers of the 1930s included Victor Stiebel, who trained at Reville and Rossiter; and Molyneux a favourite with Marina, Duchess of Kent.

For those unwilling to bear the expense of a couture designer there were the stores that boasted special dressmaking salons. Debenham and Freebody's called theirs 'Madam Paccard's Dressmaking Department' and Jays, Peter Robinson, Dickens and Jones and Harvey Nichols were among the others which had this facility. Miss Margaret Liberty Stewart had a dress from her family firm of Liberty in 1908. Thirty years later Marshall and Snelgrove supplied a gown of pale green satin with beaded ornament with a slim sleeveless fitted bodice and two floating panels from the shoulders to the bust for Lady Clanmorris. It had a salmon pink georgette train.

The service available from these stores did not stop with the sale of the dress: many offered a package, including advice and instruction on the correct way to curtsey and how to manipulate the train. Other young ladies could go to Madame Vacani's establishment at 159 Brompton Road, founded around 1916, where the basis

The last of the many, 1958, a group of debutantes arriving at Buckingham
Palace on 19 March during the last Season of presentations to the Queen.

of instruction was 'be natural, be yourself, be
unaffected'. The court curtsey when performed
in the traditional way was not too deep and
depended upon the proper placing of the knee
and the feet. It was important not to poke
forward 'look ahead of you and do not try to
assume a fixed smile. Keep your hands by your
sides and your head erect'. Madame Vacani's
lessons lasted between a half and a full hour,
depending upon the aptitude of the pupil. A
stock of long skirts and trains was kept at her

studio so that the debutantes could practice in
the sort of costume she would, eventually,
appear in.

The war of 1939–45, like the First World
War, placed a temporary halt on pesentations.
There was clearly, as after 1918, confusion as to
when and how they should be revived. But
those developments in society begun a generation earlier, were accelerated by this period of
unrest.

In 1947 20,000 debutantes were waiting to

apply for presentation. Garden Parties were arranged. The unreliable weather of an English summer soon led to these events being held in the State Apartments at Buckingham Palace. Ladies were instructed to wear 'Day dress with hat'. For many young ladies their experience of the war had brought to a head their ambivalent feelings about the world and their expectations of it. Nòel Coward seems to have anticipated the dilemma of the class in 1939.

'Four little Debutantes are we
Born of these restless changing years
Conscious of vague unwilling fears
What is our destiny to be'

In 1951 individual presentation was re-established and by the following year the revival of Evening Courts was expected. The King's death however and the accession of Elizabeth II meant that the tradition remained buried and it was Afternoon Presentation Parties that continued.

Even this echo of another age could not long survive in the post war world. On November 14 1957 the Lord Chamberlain's Office announced that 1958 would be the final year in which Presentation Parties would be held. Numbers applying for presentation had grown to such an extent that either more parties would have to be held or the whole process abandoned. In the mid-twentieth century the members of the Royal Family were already undertaking far more engagements than before and it was therefore not possible to hold more presentation parties. More people were to be invited to Garden Parties, both from the British Isles and the Commonwealth, but presentations were to end.

The Times applauded the decision. It reflected an age of social transition in Britain with traditional barriers of class breaking down. The Court was no longer the focus of an aristocracy and there were few, if any, practical advantages to be derived from presentation at Court. There were regrets. William Hickey in the *Daily Express* was saddened at the imminent departure of the court debutante although he admitted she had never been the same since before the Second World War. Inevitably there was a rush on the part of those of suitable age to be presented at Court in 1958. The last debutante to be persented was Miss Lovice Ullein Reviczky.

With the severance of the court connection the Season began to change. People wondered what sort of Season there would be without Buckingham Palace Presentations. In the event it consisted of a round of parties as before, now culminating in Queen Charlotte's Ball. This occasion was first held in 1925 with the aim of raising money for Queen Charlotte's Hospital. The ball evolved a complicated ritual which equated with the presentation ceremony which had marked the climax of the debutante's 'coming out'. The girls would congregate in an upper gallery at Grosvenor House and then process to great effect in their white dresses down a broad staircase to the ballroom floor. There they would surround a large cake, lit with a candle for each year since the death of Queen Charlotte. The girls and cake moved up the room and at a given signal the debutantes would curtsey to the guest of honour. The spectacle was described as a combination of the Nuremberg Rallies and the Dance of the Fairies in the Hall of the Mountain King. By 1977 Queen Charlotte's Ball was abandoned, victim of a changed social climate.

The opening of the Royal Academy Summer Exhibition was once looked upon as the start of the Season: few people must regard it so now. There may still be occasions such as the Henley Regatta, the Eton and Harrow Match, the Rose Ball and the Berkeley House Dress Show, at which those who consider themselves debutantes gather. Since the last presentation party at Buckingham Palace the term debutante has had little meaning, or at least, must be seen in a greatly changed context.

Perhaps only the procedure to secure admission to the Royal Enclosure at Ascot has ele-

Queen Charlotte's Ball 18 May 1968.
Debutantes parading down the staircase.

The Berkeley House Dress Show 1965. Debutantes chosen as models for the
show on the roof of Dolphin Square, London.

ments of the complicated regulations that once
determined who could appear at Court. Application for admittance has to be made in advance
to Her Majesty's Representative at Ascot, giving the name of a sponsor who has attended
previously. For ladies the wearing of a hat is still
demanded and until 1976 they could not wear
trousers. Gentlemen must wear morning dress

or uniform and although this regulation was
relaxed in 1968 to allow wearing lounge suits, so
few took advantage of this that the rules were
tightened up once more.

Court dress survives, in use, for a few appointments. There are still countries in which
British Ambassadors wear uniform. This uniform is much altered and simplified from the

days when it was a version of the Civil Uniform with additional gold embroidery on the sleeves. Governors General too wear their blue full dress or white tropical dress when appropriate. In the Palace of Westminster the Speaker of the House of Commons is still required to wear a court suit. There are a few others for whom court uniforms need not yet be consigned to the museum or saleroom but they are a greatly reduced force compared with the army that once marched to a levee in scarlet, blue, and splendid gold embroidery.

Court dress has not been prescribed for ladies since the Second World War, even for Royal Weddings and Coronations, though evening dress was worn for some years. However, many Royal wedding dresses since the one made by Hartnell for the young Princess Elizabeth in 1947 have included a long train as an important part of the ensemble—perhaps a legacy of the cumbersome court trains of earlier generations.

Yet something is missing. Clothes must be seen in a context, and that context was changed radically in 1958. The formal connection of the monarch and the Court with Society and the Season, with the Presentation as the lynchpin, has gone. Were today's 'debutantes' to wear court dress, complete with feather and veil head-dress and trains to a Society ball it would correctly be regarded as a form of fancy dress.

In the same way a Civil Uniform worn to the same function might excite amusement or amazement but it too would be no more than fancy dress.

In their day Drawing Rooms, Evening Courts and Levees had their part to play in the organization and regulation of Society and court dress and uniform were appropriate costumes, skilful blends of splendid decoration, formality, fossilization and fashion. That day has passed. But without the dresses would there have been any splendour at Court? Consider for a moment the image Thomas Carlyle conjures up in *Sartor Resartus*: 'Often when I read of Drawing Rooms [and] Levees and I strive to form a clear picture of that solemnity on a sudden as by some enchanter's hand the Clothes fly off the whole corps . . .' and where then the glittering pageant? Where then the strict etiquette?

Presented with such an image we see how important dress is to our understanding of behaviour and how inextricably linked were court etiquette and dress. As *La Belle Asemblée* remarked in 1819 'Dress shews more the manners and civilization of different states than people at a cursory glance may be led to imagine.'

Court dress as this book has shown was no exception.

The end of an era, Miss Lovice Ullein-Reviczky, the last debutante to be presented to the Queen arriving at Buckingham Palace on 20 March 1958.

GLOSSARY

AIGUILLETTE A device on a uniform distinguishing rank or office, usually consisting of gold and silver wire to which are attached needles or points. Worn from the shoulder.

ARRAS/ORRIS LACE Lace or braid woven with designs in gold or silver thread.

BOMBAZINE A fabric composed of silk and worsted which, when grey or black, was worn for mourning.

BUCKINGHAM LACE A bobbin lace made principally in the county of Buckinghamshire.

BULLION Gold or silver wire twisted to form spirals and used as trimming for certain parts of a uniform.

CHAPEAU BRAS A crescent shaped hat, carried flat under the arm.

EN GRANDE TENUE A phrase denoting the wearing of full dress.

FAILLE A fine soft corded silk.

GEORGETTE A fine semi-transparent silk.

GORGET PATCH A distinction or rank of office, consisting of patches of coloured cloth sewn to the collar of the uniform. The gorget was originally a crescent shaped piece of armour protecting the neck and from 1660–1830 officers in the British Army wore them suspended from the neck by a ribbon.

LUTESTRING A plain weave silk with lustrous finish.

MINUET A stately dance in triple measure performed by two people.

PALMETTE A design motif originally derived from the shape of a palm leaf with formalized leaves radiating outwards.

PADUA SOIE/PADUASOY A stout, plain weave silk.

SILK MOIRÉ Silk impressed with close wavy lines to give watered effect.

STOMACHER A panel roughly triangular in shape which formed the front of an open bodice, it was often decorated/a decorative feature.

TABBY A heavy silk impressed with close wavy lines to give watered effect.

TAFFETY/TAFFETA A fine glossy silk.

TOQUE A hat the design of which derives from a turban, being fitted close to the head without a brim.

SELECT BIBLIOGRAPHY

Anon, *Manners and Rules of Good Society*, 1894

Chesterfield, Earl of, *Letters to His Son*, ed Charles Strachey, 1901

Coke, Lady Jane, *Letters to Her Friend Mrs Eyre at Derby*, ed Mrs Rathoborne, 1899

Coke, Lady Mary, *Letters and Journals*, 1889–96

D'Arblay, Madame (Fanny Burney), *Diary and Letters*, ed C Barrett, 1893

Grevill, Lady Violet, *The Gentlewoman in Society*, 1892

Hervey, John Lord, *Some Materials toward Memoirs of the Reign of George II*, ed Romoney Sedgwick, 1931

Lord Chamberlain's Office, *Dress Worn at Court* (variously titled), 1882–1937

Powys, Mrs P L, *Passages from the Diary of Mrs Philip Lybbe Powys 1750–1808*, 1899

Roche, Sophie von la, *Sophie in London 1786*, 1933

Rush, Richard, *Residence at the Court of London*, ed B Rush, 1872

Saussure, C de, *A Foreign View of England in the Reigns of George I and George II*, 1902

Simond, Louis, *Journal of a Tour and Residence in Great Britain during the Years 1810–11*, 1817

Swift, Jonathan, *Journal to Stella*, ed H Williams, 1974

Thoms, William, *The Book of the Court*, 1838

Ackerman's Repository of Arts

The Graphic

Heideloff's Gallery of Fashion

Illustrated London News

La Belle Assemblée

Ladies' Magazine

Punch

The Queen

Buck, Anne, *Dress in Eighteenth Century England*, 1979

Mansfield, Alan, *Ceremonial Costume*, 1980

Millar, Sir Oliver, *Tudor, Stuart and Early Georgian Pictures in the Collection of Her Majesty the Queen*, 1963

Moreshead, Sir Owen, 'Windsor Uniforms', *Connoisseur*, May 1935

Ribeiro, A, *Dress in Eighteenth Century Europe 1715–89*, 1984

PICTURE ACKNOWLEDGEMENTS

Courtauld Institute of Art p 52 and by kind permission of Sir Brindsley Ford, CEB, FSA, p 65.

Crown copyright. Reproduced with the permission of the Controller of Her Majesty's Stationary Office p. 10, 62, 83, 85, 87, 88, 90 (both illustrations), 91 (both illustrations), 103, 107, 110, 115, 118. The publishers would also like to acknowledge the loan to the Court Dress Collection of dresses appearing in the photographs on p 62, from Cheltenham Art Gallery and Museum, on p 107 from Leicestershire Museum, Art Gallery and Record Service, on p 110 from Exeter Royal Albert Museum and on p 103 from Manchester Gallery of English Costume.

BBC Hulton Picture Library p 16, 53, 60, 68–9, 109 and 117.

Illustrated London News p 49, 75 and 123.

Kunsthistorisches Museum, Vienna p 82.

Lord Chamberlain's Office, reproduced by kind permission of Her Majesty The Queen, p 78 and 94–5.

Mary Evans/Fawcett Library p 14, 25 and 108.

Mansell Collection p 105.

Lord Middleton, by kind permission p 15.

Museum of London p 19, 20, 28, 31, 34, 42, 61, 67, 70 and 102.

National Portrait Gallery p 8, 24, 27, 56, 57, 64 (both illustrations), 71, 106, 111, 112, 113 and 116.

National Trust, Ickworth House (John Sinclair photographer) p 13.

The Photo Source p 9, 11 and 121.

Private Collections on loan to the Court Dress Collection p 29, 32, 33 (both illustrations), 36, 37, 38 (both illustrations), 39 (both illustrations), 40, 41, 44, 45, 46, 47, 50, 51, 58, 59, 63, 72, 86, 97, 98, 114 and 119.

Punch p 6, 18 and 66.

Scottish United Services Museum p 76, 77, 84, 89, 93 and 97.

Sotheby's p 54–5 and cover illustration.

Sport and General p 124.

Swaebe (Barry), photographer p 120.

Syndication International p 126.

Weybridge Museum p 101.

Windsor Castle, Royal Archives, reproduced by gracious permission of Her Majesty The Queen (copyright reserved), p 12, 21, 22, 79, 80, 96 and 104.

Victoria and Albert Museum, by courtesy of the Board of Trustees p 23, 30 and 43.

The quote in Chapter 5 taken from Nöel Coward's Debutante is by kind permission of Chappell Music Limited.